Friendly Texas Indians

And some who weren't so friendly

By Barbara Barton

Friendly Texas Indians

ISBN 978-0-967-0599-6-9

OTHER BOOKS BY BARBARA BARTON

Den of Outlaws
Stagecoach Lines and Freighters of West Texas
Pistol Packin' Preachers
Ruckus Along the Rivers
Two Feisty Schoolmarms
Ben Ficklin, Refined Pirate or Benevolent Benefactor
Secrets of the Sherwood Courthouse

Barbara Barton   (325) 656-9860
Box 6   bba7303@aol.com
Knickerbocker, TX 76939

Table of Contents

Chapter 1 The Black Seminole Indians 1

Chapter 2 The Cherokee Indians 21

Ch. 3 The Tonkawa Tribe 41

Ch. 4 Jumano Indians 69

Ch. 5 Kiowa Indians 89

Ch. 6 Lipan Indians...107

Ch. 7 Comancheros...119

Ch. 8 Comanches 133

Chapter 9 Tankersley and the Kickapoo 157

Bibliography...179

Index of Friendly Indians 187

List of Illustrations

John Gopher	5
Fort Duncan	7
Pompey Factor	8
Lt. John L. Bullis	11
Black Seminole Scouts	14
Col. Ranald Mackenzie	19
Seminole Camp	20
Cherokee cabin	22
Cherokee Chief Bowles	25
Council House	31
Chief Bowles' tombstone	40
Tonkawa Indians	42
Presidio de San Saba's gate	47
Chief Placido	52
Solstice Marker	56
Painted Rocks	57
Chief Johnson the scout	61
Tonkawa map	68
Prickly Pear plant	71
Santa Clara Pueblo	78
Salinas Pueblo Mission Natural Monument	79
Marker for Juan de Ortega and the Blue lady	87
Jumano Indian in a deer skin robe	88
Kiowa 37-month calendar	103
Chief Lone Wolf	104
Chief Kicking Bird	105
Chief Satana	106
Lipan Indian camp	108
Lipan Apache warrior	111

Indian camp drying meat   113

Sam Houston   116

Indian grinding hole   117

Mescalero Apache Chief, San Quan   118

Careta, a cart, used by Comancheros   120

Sand dune on the trail   126

Buffalo hunters   131

Cibolero ready to hunt buffalo   132

John Meusebach   144

Meusebach and Indians statue   146

Santa Anna Mountains   150

Santa Anna Stone outline of an Indian   155

Chief Yellow Wolf   156

Richard F. Tankersley   159

Annie Tankersley   164

Kickapoo wickiup   167

Tankersley house   171

Depredation Suit of R.F. Tankersley   177

Indian Shield drawing   178

Forward

I have been fascinated by the Indian tribes who lived on Texas soil for a long time, so my research evolved into this book. My interest in Texas Indians developed into an extended study of those people who helped as scouts, those who were land grant owners, and those who were friendly to all people such as the Jumano tribe in their early sojourn in this country called Texas.

At one point in the story, several Texas tribes figured into the outcome of the battle in Palo Duro Canyon, so the discussion of this battle is mentioned in the history of several different tribes. It is a reoccurring topic.

I tried to select prominent tribes who made contributions to the founding of the Texas we now enjoy. Most of the leaders I discussed attempted to help the settlers just as any neighbor would do, but the end of the story about them is quite shocking. In this book, I also included the Indians who were not so good, the ones who made life scary for early Texas settlers.

As I take pride in the actions of those early Texans called Indians, I do this partly from the fact that I am 1/16th Cherokee. My Mom knew of this bloodline on her side of the family, but as I was growing up, that topic was never discussed much. I am so relieved that in this day and time, such matters are a thing of pride. I appreciate my heritage and embrace my Indian roots.

I want to thank a friend of mine, Larry Anderson, who told me about his Cherokee ancestors; and Don Patterson who talked with me over the phone about the Tonkawa tribe in Oklahoma that he serves as President. When I ran across an article written by Rubert Richardson about an Indian scout, I felt that life had come full circle. I was blessed to be a student in his history class at Hardin Simmons University many years ago, and I think he sparked my love of history.

I have used W. W. Newcomb, Jr.'s book, *The Indians of Texas*, as a manual to guide me, as well as other good references. Many websites of Indian tribes and historians have also been very helpful in this writing effort. I decided to make one chapter of the book about the Richard Franklin Tankersley family who lived in various localities in Texas. I did this because no matter where they lived in Texas, Indians were near them at every home site.

Barbara Barton

Chapter 1 The Black Seminole Indians

Of all the Indian scouts who served in Texas, the Black Seminole Indians served as gallantly as any. But the Black Seminole scouts of Texas traveled a strange path on their way to becoming honored men of the U. S. Cavalry serving in Texas along the Rio Grande border. Many stories have been told about the black men running away from their owners in the South to seek freedom. But over time several hundred slaves managed to slip from the tyranny of their masters and escape to Florida.

Such movement of slaves to the everglades actually started before the American Revolution. The black man had been enticed to come to Florida because the Spanish in Florida delighted in getting slaves from their enemy, the British masters. An on-going fight raged between the British and the Spanish as to who could conquer the runaway slaves. The slaves were free, but according to William Loren Katz in *Black People Who Made the Old West,* the Blacks preferred to connect with the Seminole Indians rather than the Spanish.

When the black men reached the safety of Florida with all of its greenery, they discovered a new environment unlike any plantation. The swamps and everglades were scary. Alligators and snakes seemed to be the master of this environment. The runaway slaves were afraid to make contact with the Spanish living in Florida because these people might be looking for slaves of their own. A man on the run had many worries. The ex-slaves feared that their location would filter back to their owners. These new residents of Florida worried about the possibility of getting caught by the Spanish or the slave hunters. Life was lonely for the black men until they finally made contact with the Seminole Indians there in the swamps. The Spanish translation of the word "Seminole" means "runaway," so the black men were in good company. The Seminoles accepted the black men as almost equals there in the everglades of Florida.

While these black men lived in Florida, they had their own village and chief, but they stayed in contact with the

Seminoles. In fact, the Black men actually traded their white master for a Seminole master. But the Seminole treated them much better and gave them more freedom than their plantation owners did. The Seminole Indians expected the slaves to pay only a yearly tribute of food, cattle, and pelts, so the two castaways in Florida got along quite well. Some of the slaves eventually married Seminole women, so the Black Seminole Indian band evolved. The leader of these Black Seminole was a man named John Gopher. He was intelligent and wanted better things for his tribe. In 1844 a group of Seminole leaders decided to go to Washington D. C. because their homes were in jeopardy. The white man was pushing into Florida and it was obvious to the Indians that these new comers intended to push them out. Along with this delegation, John Gopher was included even though he was a Black Seminole. Word got back to the Black men in Florida that John didn't have an easy time on this trip. Some of the delegation thought he was a meddler trying to stir things up, so John was almost assassinated. But he survived and returned to Florida.

Conditions seemed to get worse, so after a while, some of the Black Seminoles decided to migrate westward. Under the direction of John Gopher in 1849, they traveled the migration trail of so many Southerners. John led about 20 Black Seminole families on a trip that took about a year, from Florida to Oklahoma and finally to Mexico. While in Oklahoma, the group made contact with the Seminole Indians there. The tired travelers hoped to stop their journey and stay in this area where several tribes lived.

The Oklahoma Seminoles liked the Black Seminoles, but they noticed that the Creeks, who also lived nearby, believed the Black Seminole were still slaves. Without their friends knowing it, the Creeks captured Black Seminole Indians and sold them as slaves. Now the black people felt that they were right back in the South where life had been full of somebody getting sold at an auction to the highest bidder. When the tribe of Black Seminoles appealed to the Indian Agents, they received no help. It was believed that the agents were actually in on the captures and the money obtained from the sale of the Black Seminoles. This predicament worried John Gopher, so he knew his group of Black Seminoles had to hit the trail again. Oklahoma wasn't going to be a good place for the Black Seminoles after all, so John Gopher moved again with his band. After traveling through hot, arid Texas, they finally settled in Northern Mexico, just across the Rio Grande in 1850. They were about equal distance from the present-day towns of Del Rio and Laredo, Texas.

The Black Seminole got along well in this new environment as well as with their new friends, the Mexicans of Coahuila. What a change in scenery they witnessed as the Rio Grande flowed through dry land filled with cactus and a few Mesquite trees. What a difference this environment was from the swamps, alligators and snakes of Florida. The Black Seminoles were later joined by more of their friends from Florida; native Seminoles, Black Creeks, and Black Cherokees. How information was sent across state lines from Florida to Mexico is a mystery, but the two groups made contact.

While the black tribe enjoyed this rugged, dry land, the Seminole Indians weren't doing so well. Many of them caught small pox and died. They lost many of their tribe, and as the years went by, they decided to return to Oklahoma to the Seminole Nation that was located there. A few of the Black Seminoles talked about going back with them, but were staunchly refused the opportunity by the Seminole chief, John Jumper. He was in charge of the Seminole Nation in Oklahoma, and he continued to tell the Black Seminole people that they hadn't been welcome when they visited several years before, and they weren't welcome now.

John Jumper presented an odd twist to the relationship between the Seminole and the Black Seminole. Both groups came from Florida where they had been pushed out of their homeland. Most of the families in the two groups got along well with each other, but John Jumper was a slave holder and supported the Confederacy. This Seminole Indian named John Jumper turned against the Black Seminoles. He said that the

3

Black Seminoles forfeited all claims on the Seminole Nation when they fled in 1850 and went to Texas. Even so, two parties of Black Seminoles did return in 1883 to Oklahoma and lived secretly in the confines of the Seminole Nation. Just as it was many years ago, the tribal status is still contested today. This controversy is discussed in *The Black Seminoles; History of a Freedom Seeking People B*y Kenneth Wiggins Porter.

But the Black Seminoles in Mexico found a different group of people lived along the Rio Grande: Mexican people. The Black Seminole travelers camped in Mexico and visited with the families living there. As the Mexicans were around the Black Seminoles more, the Mascogos they called them, the more they liked them. The Mexicans recognized the special abilities that the Seminole had, especially their leader. Since John Gopher was very good with horses, the Mexicans named him John Caballo, which means "John Horse." The Mexican government gave all the Mascogos land in exchange for their helping to protect the Mexican border. This parcel became a land grant called Hacienda el Nacimiento. Now for the first time the Black Seminole felt that they had a home.

The Mexican soldiers convinced John Horse to join the Mexican Army and fight with them against Maximillian's troops. Some big changes in Mexico's leadership had recently taken place and the men that the Black Seminole met were not happy about the new government south of the Rio Grande. The Mexican conservatives and Napoleon III gave their support to Archduke Ferdinand Maximillian and declared him emperor of Mexico on May 21, 1864. But when this move was made, Benito Juarez and his liberal forces refused to recognize Maximillian as Mexico's leader. Maximillian realized that Juarez was against him, so he tried to smooth things over by offering Benito Juarez a position in his government. Juarez staunchly refused.

As Maximillian tried to rule Mexico, his most influential supporter, Napoleon, realized that the new leader had tremendous opposition. After two years of the new emperor's shaky leadership in Mexico, Napoleon withdrew his support from Maximillian.

Gopher John, Seminole Interpreter

Gopher John was a leader of the Black Seminole who fought with the Mexican Army. Courtesy of U. S. National. Archives

The Black Seminoles found themselves in the middle of a war. John Horse was such a good soldier that he became a colonel in the Mexican Army. The soldiers called him El Coronel Juan Caballo. A Mexican saddle was a highly valued possession for a cavalryman, so the Mexican Army gave John Horse a silver-mounted saddle complete with a gold-plated pummel in the shape of a horse's head. He used this saddle for many years and rode his favorite horse "American" with the silver and gold flashing. While John Horse fought in Mexico, he had Black Seminole soldiers with him.

John Horse noticed that the Mexican President Benito Juarez befriended his people the Black Seminole, so John asked him to continue the land grant, the Mascogo Grant, for his people, and he did. In 1865 around the time that John asked Juarez to continue the grant, John was 53 years old and had lived with his wife Susan for fifteen years. They remained married until his death. When John Horse fought with Juarez, they had success and were able to capture Maximillian on May 15, 1867. The short lived rule of the Frenchman ended when he was executed.

At this time the Black Seminoles lived along the border of Texas and Mexico. While traveling across Texas, these "swamp people" probably wondered about the desert-like conditions they observed. After setting up their homes in Mexico, the scorching sun beat down on them with a vengeance. In Coahuila they scratched out a living by farming a few acres and hunting game to provide food. Remarks about the green, green grass of the home they once knew in Florida came up in conversation. They weren't satisfied with their surroundings, so eventually they moved near Fort Duncan at Eagle Pass, Texas.

Fort Duncan was up the Rio Grande on the east side of the river. As early as 1846, the Mexican War required a temporary post for U. S. troops to be present in that area. For this 4reason, Camp Eagle Pass came into existence. At that time, crude roads connected this post with Fort Inge and Fort McIntosh. The real Fort Duncan was built about the same time that the Black Seminoles came to the Rio Grande, about 1849. The infantry stationed there were involved with the trading that passed over the Rio Grande. They maintained a road for the many travelers on their way to California, as well as one they could use in their continuous scouting for Indians.

After the Civil War was over, the U. S. government took a look at the Indian problem. Especially in the eastern section of the United States, many Indian tribes were asked to leave their homeland. So many Indian tribes were moved by the United States government to the Indian Territory in Oklahoma that the Black Seminoles were wondering what was next.

Fort Duncan an early day post. Courtesy of U. S. National Archives

Surely they would probably have to do the same thing in 1870. But before they packed up their possessions to travel to Oklahoma, an unusual thing happened that affected the Black Seminole for many years. In August of that year, the United States Army made an unusual request to the tribe. Colonel Jacob De Gress, commander at Fort Duncan, sent an official invitation to the Indians to come to the fort to discuss their removal.

Black Seminole, John Kibbetts, represented his tribe in this discussion. By this time, John Horse was in his seventies, so he must have relinquished his leadership position to John Kibbetts who was about sixty years old at the time. Col. DeGress sent Captain Frank Perry of the 9th U.S. Cavalry as his emissary to talk to the Black Seminoles and see if their clan of about 200 people could come back to the United States and act as Indian scouts to help them fight the hostile tribes. Perry used Pompey Factor, a Seminole Indian to first talk to the brothers and convince them to move across the U.S. Border into the United States. Later Captain Perry crossed the Rio Grande and talked to John Kibbetts at Santa Rosa. At that meeting, a treaty was signed between the Black Seminoles and the U. S. Government.

Pompey Factor was a Black Seminole scout for the U.S. Army

It sounded like a good deal, so the tribe agreed to it. When the Black Seminoles accepted this offer, they understood that they would receive land grants in the United States for good farming land, food and provisions, as well as reimbursement for traveling costs. The band of Black Seminoles crossed the International Border July 4, 1870 and on August 18, 1870, some of the scouts were mustered into service.

Up to this time, the typical Black Seminole man dressed in bright colored hunting shirts, leggings and moccasins. They liked silver jewelry and turbans on their heads with feathery plumes added sometimes. But now these new scouts would alter their dress to blend in with the soldiers. A photograph of several Black Seminole scouts made in 1885 at Fort Clark shows the men wearing standard army pants and buttoned up jackets. The hat was the typical army felt hat with brim.

The first Muster-in Roll of ten individuals assigned to the Detachment of Seminoles Negro Indian Scouts by authority of the Commanding Officer of the Department of Texas, dated Headquarters, Department of Texas, Austin, Texas 20 July 1870 from the sixteenth of August 1870 for the term of six months unless sooner discharged. They were mustered in by Major Zenuas R. Bliss of the 25th Infantry Regiment at Fort Duncan, Texas

NAME AGE	RANK
Kibbetts, John 60	1st Sergeant
Dixie, Joe 19	Private
Factor, Dindie 21	Private
Factor, Hardie 60	Private
Factor, Pompie * 16	Private
Fay, Adams 18	Private
Kibbetts, Bobby 20	Private
Thompson, John 18	Private
Ward, John* 20	Private

Washington, George	Private
21	
Wood, John	Private
60	

*Subsequently awarded the Medal of Honor. Four of these soldiers, Adam Paine, Isaac Payne, John Ward, and Pompey Factor are buried in the nearby cemetery. They received their honors for riding with the Seminole Negro Indian Scouts. A fifth metal of Honor recipient, Claron "Gus" Windus, is also buried there, and he served with the all white 6th Cavalry. Gus Windus was also a deputy sheriff of Kinney County.

While the first scouts were living at Fort Duncan, they became trackers for Major Bliss because they could usually find the trail of the enemy he was following. They did their job so well that he increased the scouts to a total of 31 in 1871. Up to this point, the scouts had to furnish much of their equipment used, but Major Bliss changed the Black Seminole scouts to permanent military status. This advancement meant that the Indian scouts received arms, ammunition, and rations as well as the standard pay for a private in the army. John Kibbetts received slightly more since he had the duties of sergeant. In today's world, their pay seemed very small. A private in the U. S. Army during the Civil War received $13 a month. Since most of the men had never received pay of any kind, the money probably looked pretty good.

From 1870 to 1873, more Black Seminoles came from their home in Mexico at Matamoros, Tamaulipas, or Laguna de Parras to live near Fort Duncan. By the end of this time, the population of Black Seminoles numbered 180. The Black Seminole scouts were making a name for themselves as being very efficient, so Lt. Col. Wesley Merrit wanted some of the scouts transferred to Fort Clark. When they made this move in July of 1872, they not only had a new home but also a permanent leader. Lt. John Lapham Bullis would now lead the scout group. Lt. Bullis was a young white officer, only thirty-two-years-old, and very inexperienced.

Lt. John L. Bullis was a leader and friend to the Black Seminole soldiers.

He never had worked with Indians as scouts. Some people around the fort wondered if the green officer would have a terrible time with the Indians. What the soothsayers didn't know was that Bullis had the right attitude. When they were scouting far from the comforts of the fort, Bullis endured the same hardships as his men did. He took no special privileges when they were on patrol. When he returned to the fort, Bullis was interested in the welfare of his men's families. He acted as a go-between when matters of the family surfaced. Not long after Lt. Bullis took over the Black Seminole scouts, Col Ranald S. Mackenzie came into the area fighting hostile Indians. In May of 1872, he had Bullis and his men help him in a raid near El Remolino, Coahuila. He wanted to attack the Kickapoo camp without the Mexicans knowing about his raid. The Kickapoo camp was forty miles into the interior of Mexico, so the scouts had to keep the U.S. forces away from any Mexican troops. Mackenzie attacked the Indians successfully and got back over the border before the wrong people saw him. He was impressed with the Black Seminole scouts because he asked for their help again when he led a force into Palo Duro Canyon two years later.

The Palo Duro Canyon Battle was the major battle in the Red River War. It pitted the federal troops against the Apache, Kiowas, Cheyenne, and Comanche warriors. All of these tribes agreed to meet and camp in the canyon by late September of 1874. The Kiowa shaman, Mayran, promised all the Indians would be safe. But they didn't know the tenacity of Col. Mackenzie. When he started a campaign, he finished it. His men arrived at the canyon September 24, 1874 and he was depending on his guide, Tonkawa Chief Johnson and his Black Seminole scouts to access the situation. This evasion of the rugged canyon homes of so many Indians was a big undertaking. The Seminole Scouts had to travel to a part of Texas that was about 450 miles from their home where their families lived near Fort Clark. The scouts wore several hats on this campaign. They were expected to track the enemy, which were Comanches, Cheyennes and Kiowas; to act as couriers between different military groups; and prepare to fight for their lives.

When the Black Seminoles reached the edge of the Palo Duro Canyon, they were told to search for other Indian bands. Soon the scouts returned from their snooping around and let the soldiers know that the Indians were in about three big groups scattered throughout the Palo Duro Canyon. They were led by Cheyenne Chief Iron Shirt, Comanche Chief Poor

Buffalo, and Kiowa Chief Lone Wolf. The three tribes were camped far enough apart that the U.S. Army fought three different battles.

Each tribe was chased out of the canyon and forced to leave most all of their belongings behind. The escaping Indians ran across the rugged area with hills and canyons but left their horses because they were in such disarray they didn't have time to get them. Indians left their cooking pots and supplies strung along the canyon floor. For such a big number of fighters, there were only three Indians and one white man killed. Since Tonkawa Chief Johnson was also a guide for the army, he carried some Tonkawa people with him on the trip, including some women, when he searched the Indian camps. The women enjoyed pilfering through the defeated Indians' teepees. The Tonkawa took what they could carry of their loot and destroyed the rest of the Comanche' property that they were forced to leave behind.

U. S. soldiers captured 1,400 Indian ponies. Chief Johnson was given forty of them, and the Black Seminole Scouts received 300 horses. In order to make the defeated Indians even more helpless, the army shot the rest of the unwanted horses found in the canyon. After this battle settled the Red River War, the Black Seminole Scouts found themselves handling a different kind of problem.

From 1875 to 1881, the Black Seminole scouts spent most of their time tracking small raiding parties who were running from the Indian Reservations or from their hiding places along the Rio Grande. One fight the Seminole scouts were a part of happened half-way between the two retreats. They were in a fight at Eagle Nest Creek on the Pecos River. This location is where highway 90 crosses the Pecos River. On April 25, 1875, Bullis and three scouts tracked about 25 to 30 Indians for four days. The Indians' trail was a wide enough swath that their trackers knew they had close to 75 horses with them. Bullis and his three scouts: Factor, Payne, and Ward, waited until the Indians camped. Then they crept up close to the camp and opened fire.

13

Left to right: Billy July, Ben July, Denbo Factor and Ben Wilson at Ft. Clark about 1885. Courtesy of Charles Downing.

The scouts and the Indians fought for about 45 minutes until the Indians pulled a neat trick on them. They flanked the soldiers and then started a counter-attack. Bullis ordered a retreat. The three scouts mounted and rode off only to realize that Bullis wasn't with them. They returned to find him alone with no mount. His horse had run away before he could catch him. Bullis was under heavy fire when the scouts returned. Factor and Payne provided cover fire while Ward rode to Bullis, pulled him up on the horse, and speed away. After this battle,

14

the following Black Seminole scouts earned the Medal of Honor: John Ward, Isaac Payne, and Pompey Factor. Pvt. Adam Payne had already won this award for his gallantry in the Red River War.

Not all scouting work was accomplished in the saddle. The well-known Seminole scouts also helped build roads where military supplies and equipment could be pulled over it easier. Bullis decided a wagon road needed to be shortened between Fort Clark and Fort Davis. This could be done by blasting a road into Pecos Canyon near the Rio Grande. The canyons were very deep with steep walls in this area, so his Seminole scouts did the impossible by going through the canyon wall. This road work was completed after the Civil War.

It sounds like everything was going well for the scouts, but they had some other problems. An outlaw named John King Fisher operated around Brackettville, which was a town very close to Fort Clark. John King Fisher was a big time cattle rustler, and he had a gang of Mexicans who helped him. The way they both looked at rustling was that each would help the other. King Fisher smuggled cattle from Texas across the border to Mexico while his Mexican friends brought him cattle they had smuggled from Mexico.

King Fisher dressed the part of a Mexican outlaw. He wore a big Mexican sombrero with golden braid, a silk shirt, and crimson sash. He carried a silver mounted holster with ivory handled, silver plated pistols. After the cattle had been sold, King Fisher distributed the money to each gang member. However, sometimes the argument ensued when they didn't think King Fisher was giving them enough. He was known to have killed several gang members who disagreed with him. Finally King Fisher made enough money to buy himself a ranch near Eagle Pass. He seemed to be settling down, but he was still arrested several times for gambling. King Fisher became sheriff of the county for a time, he got married, and he had several children. But his wild ways got the best of him. At the young age of thirty he was killed in a gunfight.

Some of the Black Seminoles had some encounters with King Fisher's gang because they were trying to push the Seminole Indians from their home. On May 18, 1876, John Horse and Titus Payne had enjoyed a drink at a saloon near Fort Clark. At the end of the day, they started home and their path led near the Fort Clark Cemetery. At that moment shots rang out and Titus fell from his horse. He was dead. Then four shots hit John Horse and his horse, American. They were both badly wounded but they made it home. Who actually fired these shots has been much debated.

No one was ever apprehended for the murder of Titus, but most people felt it was the work of King Fisher's men. It was a well-known fact that King Fisher hated the Seminole Scouts, but nobody would testify against him. One time Fisher killed Scout George Washington in a barroom brawl, and he never was tried for the murder. Fisher had such an iron grip on Kinney County that no one would be a part of a grand jury to indict him.

This episode marked the fourth time that John Horse had experienced an attempt on his life, so the Seminole Community was very upset. If Fisher's men didn't do the shooting, some people argued that, it might have been some of the white people who didn't want the Seminoles to farm the good land along the Los Moras River. During the fall of 1876, the Black Seminole community was worried and upset. They were afraid that other Seminoles might be killed, they were hungry from lack of supplies, and they began to argue with each other. Even the white people in Brackettville argued. Some people thought the Seminoles were thieves while others thought the Seminole scout group needed to be increased so Lt. Bullis would have more help controlling the hostile Indians and bandits in the area.

Into this caldron of unrest rode Sheriff L. C. Crowell and his deputy, Claron "Gus" Windus. Gus was the more colorful of the two lawmen. He ran away from home in Wisconsin at the young age of 13. He served awhile as drummer and then Union soldier before serving time for stealing horses in 1867.

By 1870 Gus was soldering in Texas and fighting Kicking Bird and the Kiowa Indians in the Battle of the Little Wichita River. His fellow soldiers were almost wiped out by the Kiowa, so he made it through the enemy lines and brought help. He was given a Medal of Honor for his bravery. By July of 1875, Gus Windus arrived in Brackettville and soon wore the title of deputy sheriff.

Now in the fall of 1876, Gus found himself right in the middle of a big disagreement between the Black Seminole and the community near them. Suddenly the indictments against fellow Seminoles began to accumulate. The first thing that happened was August Scout was accused of stealing five horses in August of 1876. Then a month later, Isaac Payne and Dallas Griner were indicted because they supposedly stole a well-bred gelding that just happened to belong to Deputy Sheriff Windus. Payne and Scout waded over the Rio Grande and spent time in Nacimiento, Mexico away from Windus.

Everything would have been alright if the accused men had stayed across the border, but New Years Eve celebrations were important to the Black Seminole community, so all the accused men made their way back home as they stealthily crossed the river. Sheriff Crowell and Deputy Windus knew about the celebration that night in the Black Seminole community, so when it reached it noisiest climax, Deputy Windus shot Adam Paine with a shot gun at close range. Frank Enoch was also mortally wounded. Isaac Payne and Dallas Griner got away while Bobby Kibbett jumped the lawmen to keep them from shooting anybody else.

The Black Seminole Indians continued to have problems. Black Seminole Indians lived on land around Fort Clark that some white families wanted, and they wouldn't let the Indians forget this fact. The troublemakers wanted the scouts moved, so the land could go up for public sale. John Bullis had always looked out for the best interest of his scouts. Now he was transferred in 1882 to Indian Territory. When he left, there was nobody who would go to bat for the scouts and their families. Before he left, the scout group had numbered about fifty men. Now this number was slashed as well as the rations given to the scouts' families.

When the soldier friends of the Black Seminole scouts heard of their problems, they lobbied to Congress for help. Men who took the Indians' side of the problem were John Bullis, Mackenzie, Col. Edward Hatch, and even Gen. Philip H. Sheridan, commander of the Military Division of the Missouri. Surely with all of these men fighting in their behalf, the scouts would have gotten some help.

But no, they received no aid. Some Seminoles such as Pompey Factor decided to give up his job as scout and move to Mexico for good in 1880. He, like many others, farmed for many years in Mexico. Some Indians succeeded and others returned to the U.S. to ask for a pension from the army. Factor didn't receive his pension before he died, so he was buried in the Scout's cemetery in 1928.

The Black Seminoles lost their land they were living on, and then in 1912 they lost their scouting jobs. The last Black Seminole scout was mustered out of the army in August of 1912. According to a letter sent August 18, 1932, from Congressman J.H. Brooks, Assistant Secretary of Indian Affairs to the Commissioner of Indian Affairs, there may have been a treaty stating they should have reparations. The Black Seminoles had stayed on their reservation from 1870 until 1913. According to this letter, in 1913 Col. Shelby of the 13th Cavalry visited the Black Seminoles and asked to see the original treaty between the Black Seminoles and the government. The Indians felt that they had left the treaty in Santa Rosa, Mexico, so they sent John Shields, a first Sergeant back to get the treaty. A Mexican Revolution was going on in that part of Mexico. Before they could retrieve any papers, the courthouse at Santa Rosa was destroyed in the Revolution. With its demise the papers of the treaty were lost.

This 1932 letter to Congressman Brooks was answered by Acting Commissioner Garber. He implied that if the Black Seminole Indians had any rights, they lost them when they left the Seminole Indian Nation in Oklahoma. He said these rights were closed under the Act of April 26th, 1906. He also said that according to his records he thought the Black Seminole scouts possessed very little Indian blood.

Through the years, other historians have tried to find the paper treaty but had no luck. Most of the Black Seminole families moved to nearby Brackettville, Del Rio or Eagle Pass. Others went to adjoining border towns and eked out a living as ranch hands, laborers, and domestic servants. Their courageous service to the U. S. Army was largely forgotten, and they received no land from the treaty they believed they made with the U. S. government.

But to this day, many descendants of the Black Seminoles scouts live in Kinney County or in Brackettville.

Col. Ranald Mackenzie used Black Seminole scouts. Courtesy of West Texas Collection, Angelo State University

Seminole camp near Fort Clark. From Robert N. Dennis Collection. The living conditions of most Black Seminoles was in rustic housing such as this.

Chapter 2 The Cherokee Indians

As the young man moved through the forest of western North Carolina, an observer would certainly notice his flaming red hair and freckles on his tanned face. But when he turned in the trail to go home, he didn't enter the settler's village. Home for him was a Cherokee settlement with summer homes built in a square framework of poles. The outside of his house was probably covered with bark, or woven siding to keep it cool during the hot months.

This young hunter named Duwali Bowles didn't look exactly like a typical Cherokee boy although he was accepted into the tribe. His ruddy complexioned Scotch-Irish father married his Cherokee mother and Duwali was born in 1756 in the town called Little Hiwasee. His father was thought to have come to the area as an Indian trader and continued to move among the various tribes. Bowles' father was one among the many Scottish men who came to America to trade with the American Indians in the 1700s. The traders wanted deerskins, beaver hides, and other pelts that could be made into leather by the European factories.

Such men from the Highland region of Scotland were a little on the wild side. They loved sports or any outside activity, and dressed similar to the Indians. Mr. Bowles must have had a short temper because over the years, some bad blood developed between him and men in a nearby settlement. The Scot was mysteriously killed by his enemies. Duwali lost his father when he was only fourteen years of age. The young Cherokee mourned over his Father's death and then took action. He promptly murdered the men who were to blame. From that time onward, Duwali was considered to be a young leader in their Cherokee band.

When Bowles was in his thirties, he was Chief of the Cherokee band who was living in Running Water, Tennessee. Originally most of the Cherokee families were farmers, but they moved about so much that they no longer supported themselves. Because the Cherokee were not use to these hills and streams, they hadn't found a place to settle permanently.

For the first time, these proud Cherokee depended on the government to give them supplies. One time Chief Bowles and his band showed up at the appointed time and received their allotment at the government post in Tennessee. This routine had been normal for them to get the supplies and return to their camp.

A Cherokee Cabin in North Carolina. Courtesy of the U.S. National Archives.

But this time, they met someone on the way home. As they traveled back to their camp, a man named William Scott called to the Indians from his boat anchored on the nearby river. He asked them if they wanted to trade with him. Although the Cherokees didn't know Scott, they walked down to the dock where his boat was tied. Scott's barge was filled with trade goods plus five other men, three women, four children and twenty slaves.

The Cherokee Indians traded their new supplies that they had just received for things that Scott had on the boat, which were really just trinkets. While planning some trickery, Scott offered the Indians some whiskey. When they drank enough to be drunk, the traders took all the supplies that the Indians had just received. The Indians were helpless until the effect of the liquor disappeared.

Bowles and the others eventually sobered up to find they had lost most of their supplies that they had been issued. The Cherokee were upset when they fully realized what they had lost, so they searched for William Scott and his boat. The trader hadn't traveled very far down the river, so Bowles and his men caught up with the slow moving barge. The Indians talked to Scott and tried to reason with the traders. According to Cherokee folk lore, they asked the traders that their valuable supplies be returned. The white men refused, so Bowles asked them a second time. When the traders refused to return the supplies to the Cherokee again, the Indians went on a rampage and killed all the men. The wives and children of the dead men saw the bloody action take place before their eyes, so they feared for their lives too.

Surely they wondered if they would also be killed. But Bowles and his men respected the defenseless women, so they took the remaining white women, children, and slaves to safety. The Indians didn't lift a hair from the head of the children or their mothers, but they reasoned that killing these traders would probably bring them a lot of trouble. The Cherokee felt that the authorities would be chasing them soon anyway.

Chief Bowles knew his braves and himself were in trouble for killing the settlers, so they packed up their important items. They left Tennessee and moved toward Missouri. In 1809 they crossed the Mississippi River and found a home near the old Spanish trading post of New Madrid. Once they settled in this home in Southern Missouri, they planted their fields and built their homes. Their houses resembled log cabins of other settlers in the 1800s. As the Cherokee planted their crops and maintained them, the tribe grew much larger over time. Families prospered and their children had families also. Eventually Bowle's group was called the Cherokee Nation West. All was going well for the Cherokee until Missouri experienced several scary earth tremors in 1811 and 1812. This phenomenon was later called the New Madrid Earthquake, and it definitely got the attention of the Indians as well as anybody else living in the four-cornered region where Missouri, Arkansas, Kentucky and Tennessee meet.

The Earthquake was first recorded at 2:15 on the morning of December 16, 1811. And another tremor hit six hours later. Houses were damaged and chimneys toppled. John Bradbury was on the Mississippi that night, and said he was awakened by a loud noise. His boat was shaking and trees were falling into the river. Although the Cherokee would have noticed a tremendous amount of damage in the forest around them, they remained in their village. However, on January 23, 1812, another tremor was felt in the same area. This event was only 38 days after the first earthquake. People complained about the earth moving, severe landslides occurring, and stream banks caving off into the river.

The Cherokee believed these tremors were a curse, so they pulled together their belongings and traveled southwestward into Arkansas, far enough they hoped that they would be safe from the "shaking earth." They stayed there until 1817, but the U.S. Government had new ideas. They demanded that all Indians move to an area between the White and Arkansas Rivers. Chief Duwali Bowles had a meeting and his council decided they wouldn't go where the government dictated. Instead he wanted to move further west, so he took his sixty warriors and their families into Tejas country. Texas, as this country was later called, was controlled by the Spanish at this time. The Spanish were eager to have the Indians on the eastern side of Tejas country, so they could slow down the influx of settlers.

Duwali and his tribe were very traditional Cherokee. When they left Tennessee, they didn't take up the liberal ways of the old tribe. According to D. C. Utsidihi Hicks in his "History of the Texas Cherokee," the Tejas tribe practiced Clan Law and the ancient religious beliefs and customs of their ancestors." When voting on leaders took place, women as well as men had a vote. Up to this time, several Cherokee chiefs managed the tribe, but in Texas, Bowles became Ugu or head chief. Sometimes he served as both War Chief and as Head Chief at the same time because the tribe believed in his leadership. But on other occasions, the tribal history shows that they also had a War Chief.

Chief Duwali Bowles, the Cherokee leader in Texas. Courtesy of the Texas State Library & Archives Commission.

When Bowles directed his clan to Texas he didn't know that the Comanche, Apache and other Plains Indians already controlled Texas. At first, the Cherokee settled on the Trinity River near Dallas, but quickly ran into the aggressive Plains Indians. Whereas the Cherokee built cabins and farmed the land, the Plains Indians migrated wherever the Buffalo and game moved. They had no settlement where they made permanent homes. The Apache and Comanche could move quickly from one site to another because their tepees could be dismantled and ready to travel in a short time. War cries soon echoed around the Cherokee settlements because the Comanche attacked with a vengeance. Wars with the Plains Indians caused the Cherokee to lose a third of their braves to these militant tribes in a rather short time.

The Cherokee found themselves moving again, much to their chagrin. Chief Bowles' next move was to the pine forests of East Texas. He settled his people north of Henderson and not far from the eastern border of Texas. The leaders of the tribe asked the Mexicans for a title to their land in this area. This decision was obviously due to them losing their homes in the eastern states. The Indian council believed if they had a deed to their property, they would not be pushed off of it. In a way, this tribe was trying to play by the rules, and obtain deeds to their property so they could live near the other settlers peacefully. These Indians had a long history of owning their farms, building towns, and educating their children, so they didn't think of themselves as inferior to the other settlers who came westward to settle near them.

After much duress, the Cherokee received titles to their land, but the titles weren't very clear. The tribe grew in numbers because they banded together with twelve weaker tribes in Texas. Soon they formed the coalition called "Cherokees and Their Associate Bands." Some of the other tribes came from eastern areas like the Cherokee did. They were looking for a home and for safety. The group raised livestock and farmed so well that they actually sold corn to some people living around Nacogdoches. Since it was the largest town in that area, the Cherokee had a ready market.

When the Mexicans won their independence from Spain in 1823, the Mexican government affirmed the rights of all these Indian tribes to live in Texas. These tribes were working and living together peacefully, so the new government wanted to keep these peaceful Indians happy. The new government also appointed an Indian Agent to work with the tribes. A hero of the

Mexican army named Peter Ellis Bean was tabbed for this position.

Now Peter Bean was a colorful character who worked both sides of the fence for his benefit. As a 17 year old, he left his home in Bean Station, Tennessee to join Philip Nolan's trip to seek wealth in Texas. Although the fortune seekers had a fortified camp in the McLennan or Hill County region, Spanish troops killed Nolan and captured Peter Bean and other survivors. After this reversal of fortune, Bean found himself on the road to Mexico on March 22, 1801. Bean and his friends were placed in a Mexican prison. He endured prison conditions for nine years before a priest, Jose Maria Morelos y Pavon, pitied the young prisoner and helped him escape. Bean fought with the priest and his revolutionary army after he found freedom. For the next 20 years Bean served with the Mexican army and then with Jackson's army in New Orleans. By 1823, he decided to settle down with his family in East Texas. At this point he was appointed Indian Agent for the Cherokee.

Most white settlers liked the hard working Cherokee and got along with them well into the 1830s when the Texas Revolution took place against Mexico. A prominent character in Texas leadership was a person from Tennessee. Some of the Cherokee knew this leader named Sam Houston many years before they moved to Texas. Sam Houston was born March 2, 1793 near Lexington, Virginia, and his father died when he was fourteen. Soon afterward, Sam and his mother moved to Blout County, Tennessee. His older brothers helped him get a job clerking in a trader's store, but the outdoors called to him, so he ran away to live with some Cherokee friends. John Jolly, a mixed blood Cherokee, had hunted in the forest with Sam and taught him the Indian's way to love nature and have endurance when needed. They also played Indian games together. One time Sam and Jolly quarreled. Sam hit Jolly, but the Cherokee boy soon forgot the incident, and years later John Jolly was interviewed about his relationship with Houston. Jolly said he was still a friend Sam's.

After three years with the Cherokee, Sam returned to civilization and taught in a small school. In 1817 he was asked to be a sub-agent to help move the Cherokee to Arkansas. Houston made a mistake one day when he appeared before John C. Calhoun, Secretary of War. Sam Houston was dressed in Indian garb. Calhoun rebuked Sam for wearing the clothes of an Indian, so Houston resigned his position with the government in 1818. At that point, Houston wasn't Secretary of War. He came back home to live a normal life and find a wife. Sam Houston finally went through matrimony with Eliza Allen. But when his marriage didn't work out with Eliza in January of 1829, he returned to live with the Cherokee.

On his trip back "home," Sam Houston discovered that the Cherokees who remained on their land in the eastern states were having lots of problems. Settlers wanted the fertile land owned by the Cherokee, and the government seemed to be siding with the settlers. Finally the Cherokee Council filed a law suit with the United States government asking them to remove the settlers and let them keep land that had been plowed and planted by the Cherokee Nation for many years.

In the early years of existence, the Cherokee Nation covered a large area. It included more than half of Tennessee, much of southern Kentucky, the southwestern corner of Virginia, a large part of the two Carolinas, a large section of Georgia, and the northern region of Alabama. It was estimated to be at least 6,000 acres at one time. But as the white settlers pushed westward, they encroached on the Cherokee property. Sometimes the Cherokee villages were burned to the ground by people who wanted their rich land. Finally the Cherokee went to Washington and filed a case against the state of Georgia for encroaching on their farms. The Cherokee men who represented their tribe and visited the capital in Washington were dressed much like other men in suits of the day's fashion complete with white shirts. The Cherokee delegation included two men in their twenties, John Ridge and William Cooley, and the older statesman, Richard Taylor.

As this delegation talked with Pres. Andrew Jackson that July day in 1831, he told them they had lost their suit against Georgia. Although Jackson appreciated the Cherokee fighting with him in earlier days when he was a U.S. soldier, now he was President of the United States. He looked at situations differently and turned against the Cherokee delegation. He told them that they would never win back their property. In *The American Story Defiant Chiefs*, produced by Time-Life Books, Jackson's cool words to the Cherokee were, "You can live on your lands in Georgia if you choose, but I cannot interfere with the laws of that state to protect you." Soon after that meeting, many Cherokee were forced to sell their land while others voluntarily sold theirs, but the Cherokee who had migrated toward the west, owned very little land.

Although Andrew Jackson was known for his bluster and stern nature as a soldier, it's hard to imagine him being so heartless toward his Indian friends who had fought with him. To take this idea one step further, Andrew Jackson had three adopted sons, two of which were Indians. Theodore was one Indian adopted son; Lyncoya was a Creek Indian that he adopted after the Creek War, and Andrew Jackson, Jr. was his third adopted son. Andrew was the son of Mrs. Jackson's brother, Severn Donelson. The Jacksons were guardians to eight other children. Three of these children had parents who were once friends of the Jackson family and five of the children were offspring of the Jackson's relatives. Although Jackson seemed to have a heart, he left the Cherokee out in the cold.

The Indians who had tried to work out their problems in the courts like the white men did were bewildered at the outcome of their trip to Washington. One Cherokee Chief was particularly upset by the treatment they received from Pres. Jackson because he had fought by his side in years past. This chief was heard to say that it was too bad that he didn't shoot the S.O.B. when he had the chance.

When the Cherokee leaders returned home, they were uncertain as to what they should do. Chiefs like Duwali Bowles had left the eastern states some years ago, but the majority of the Cherokee Nation remained in their homes. Over the course of the next several years, the Cherokee were attacked repeatedly and told to leave. Finally the United States Congress ratified a law that said they must leave. While the eastern Cherokee packed their bags and were driven from their property, Chief Bowles was having his own brand of trouble in Texas. But he did have one government representative in Texas that considered his side of the story.

Sam Houston was very active in politics when the Cherokee came to Tejas country. Houston was known as a man who spoke up for Indian rights both in 1830 and 1832. In both cases he was exposing fraudulent practices against the Cherokee, so President Jackson sent him to Texas in December of 1832 to negotiate treaties with the Texas Indians. American traders had asked Jackson specifically for help along the border of Texas. Up until this point, the Cherokee believed that maybe Jackson would take their side in Texas disagreements, but it didn't work out that way.

Chief Bowles knew it was important to own your land and hoped that his tribe would settle down to do that. He understood the laws well enough that he petitioned for a land grant soon after he arrived in Texas. From this decision we know that Bowles was trying to play this game of controlling land by the white man's rules. He sent diplomatic chief Richard Fields to Mexico in hopes that he could negotiate a land treaty with the Mexican government. Richard Fields, born in 1780, was only an eighth Cherokee, but his diplomatic skills were noticed early in life. He was just twenty-one years old when he was chosen emissary of the Cherokee council to United States agents in Tennessee. Fields was listed as an interpreter on September 19, 1812 at the Council House treaty council in Chickasaw country. Two years later he served as captain of a Cherokee unit who were attached to Gen. Andrew Jackson's army in the War of 1812. Richard Fields eventually made his way to Tejas country and was a leader of one of the several Cherokee villages scattered over East Texas.

When the Cherokee Council decided they wanted to obtain land grants from the Spanish government, they sent for Richard Fields. He could speak English, so the Council felt he could tell the Spanish which land they wanted. In November of 1822, Richard Fields and twenty-two Cherokee made their way to San Antonio. On November 8, 1822 the group met with Lieutenant Governor of the Province of Tejas, Jose Felix Trespalacios. He gave them an "Articles of Agreement" that provided them with land. In return, the Cherokee were to help the Spanish armies control the number of "Yankee Anglos" flooding into Tejas.

Council House where treaties were signed. Courtesy of U.S. National Archives

This agreement seemed to have set well with the Cherokee because if they acted as policemen, they could keep any unwanted migrants from taking their farms.

But before the Cherokee could put this treaty into action, the Spanish government was overthrown and Tejas country came under Mexican government rule. The new government tried to pacify the Cherokee by naming Chief Bowles as a lieutenant colonel in the Mexican army.

Shortly after this failed attempt by the Cherokee to get land grants, two brothers, Haden and Benjamin Edwards, entered Texas. They first appeared in East Texas near Nacogdoches. These white settlers also wanted acreage for themselves, so they appealed straight to the Mexican government for a land grant near Nacogdoches. When they arrived at the location of their new farm, they found that other Texans had already occupied it. But when these settlers who were already living on their land protested to the Mexican government, the Edwards grants were revoked. Benjamin Edwards decided to organize his own army and claim the land as the Independent Republic of Fredonia.

Edwards organized a government and made a treaty with a few Cherokee on behalf of the Republic of Fredonia on December 16, 1826. Copies of the treaty can still be found. Richard Fields, the Cherokee diplomat, and John D. Hunter, a white man, signed the treaty on behalf of the Cherokee. This decision was made at first with the approval of all the Cherokee Council. But the more the Cherokee observed the conflict between Edwards and the Mexicans government, the more the Council decided to reverse their decision to fight with Benjamin Edwards. The Cherokee tribe finally took the Mexican side of the battle at Fredonia. Indian Agent Peter Bean talked to the Cherokee during this conflict and told them to stay neutral. Most of the Cherokee followed his suggestion.

But some of the Indians such as Richard Fields decided to fight with John Hunter. As the plans for a fight continued, the Republic of Fredonia looked for protection in some building. There existed a stone fort in the area north of Nacogdoches, so Edwards and his men, along with the some Indians, seized this fort to protect themselves. About 60 men, mostly Mexicans rode into Nacogdoches planning to attack the fort and get it back in the right hands, but they were routed by Edwards and his men. Richard Fields and John Hunter were on their own as they fought on the side of the Republic of Fredonia and Benjamin Edwards. Those two Cherokee were not supported by any other Cherokee warriors in this fight. Even though Edwards and his group won that battle, he decided he couldn't fight the whole Mexican army, so he dissolved his republic and fled to Louisiana. The Republic of Fredonia vanished as quickly as it was ordained.

Bowles' warriors fought alongside the Mexicans to squelch the Fredonia Rebellion. For this reason, the Indians were hopeful they would receive land grants from the Mexicans. But the leaders of the Cherokee tribe had another problem on their hands: what to do with Fields and Edwards who had fought against the Mexicans? The Cherokee had a council to decide the fate of their Indian brother, Richard Fields, and his companion, John Hunter, who fought against the Mexicans. Fields was part Indian, but at the council, both men were convicted of going against the Cherokee Council in their support of Edwards.

Somehow both of the condemned men escaped from the Cherokee camp after they were convicted. Fields and Hunter high-tailed it to parts unknown, both hoping they could out run their troubles. Fields was on the way to Louisiana where his brother and father lived, but he was caught just inside the Texas border. Hunter found protection in an Anadarko Indian town, but when the Cherokee warriors found him, the Anadarko people refused to help the condemned man. Both Indian tribes lived by the same code. They wouldn't contradict the decision of another tribe's council, so each man was executed in February of 1827 by Chief Bowles' tribe. The Mexican Government thanked the Cherokee for taking care of the problem so quickly.

Although no land grants appeared after Bowles helped the Mexican soldiers, events took place that made it seem likely to the Cherokee that the land would soon come from not the

Mexican government but the State of Texas and their new government.

This turn of events hinged on a friendship. The Cherokee people kept in contact with their friend, Sam Houston, and told him they wanted land. Several years later, Sam Houston was able to negotiate a settlement where the Cherokee tribes would have 1.5 million acres north of the Old San Antonio Road. This piece of property lay between the Neches River on the west and the Angelina River as its eastern boundary in Texas. The slice of land they received included these modern-day towns: Rusk, Alto, and Lufkin. In order to make this agreement official, 54 delegates who represented Texas signed the agreement between Texas and the Cherokee tribes. This decision must have made the Cherokee people very happy, because they now had a land deed. Surely this tribe felt that they couldn't be removed from their land in Texas like they had been removed earlier in the eastern states.

But when the war for Texas Independence ended, and Texas had its own Congress, a very strange thing happened. The Texas Legislature refused to honor the Treaty of 1837, which they had made with the Indians. Bowles and his Cherokee tribe were left empty handed again with no land.

To make matters worse for the Indians, Sam Houston by Texas law couldn't run again for the position of President of Texas, so the Indians had no spokesperson to stand up in their behalf in government issues. In 1838, The Republic of Texas elected Mirabeau Bonaparte Lamar as president. Suddenly the attitude towards Indians changed, partly because Lamar had a different background than Houston did. Lamar, born in Georgia in 1798, grew up reading, writing poetry, and preparing to be in the legislature. By the age of 31, he was elected to the Georgia Senate. But the loss of his wife Tabitha to tuberculosis in 1830 sent Lamar in a spiral downward. He couldn't get interested in any of his former ventures, so he came to Texas to visit his friend James Fannin. He landed in Texas just in time to get involved in their war. After fighting in the battle of San Jacinto, Lamar was elected vice-president of Texas.

It wasn't very long after Lamar took office that he expressed his hatred for Indians. He had no plans like Houston did to assimilate them into Texas' future. While Sam Houston took a long trip back to Tennessee after he stepped down from his Texas leadership, President Lamar formulated his plan. Lamar told his Texas Commissioners and Army to speak to the Indian tribes. His message to the Indians was that they were to depart from Texas or they would be removed by force. Lamar detached two companies of soldiers to occupy the Neches Saline so they could keep an eye on the Cherokee. Neches Saline was a town in southwest Smith County, so the Cherokee had stayed in the deep piney woods of East Texas up to this point. If a person expects bad behavior from somebody, they usually can find it. In a short period of time, events took place that put the Cherokee in a bad light. When a Mexican emissary named Flores was killed in a skirmish, soldiers found a letter on him that was meant for Chief Bowles. Supposedly the letter suggested that Bowles was in contact with Mexican officials and probably wanting to join them. When Sam Houston was told about the letter, he wasn't convinced that the Cherokee were trying to take sides with the Mexicans.

At this time, President Lamar and his staff felt that the Cherokees should be removed from Texas. As they made their plans of expulsion, Lamar called upon Brigadier General Albert Sidney Johnston, to arrange for their dismissal. Johnston had completed a quick rise through the army ranks of Texas. After he graduated from West Point, he lost his young wife to tuberculosis in 1836. He resigned from his position in the United States Army and headed to Texas. There he found war between Texas and Mexico brewing. Soon he was involved in the battles and rose quickly up the ranks to General. Now Pres. Lamar wanted him to chase the Indians out of Texas. Martin Lacy, the Indian agent for Texas was first sent to talk to Chief Bowles. At this time, the Cherokee lived about 2.5 miles northwest of what is now called the town of Alto in present-day Cherokee County. This new home was a few miles south of where they had been living since coming to East Texas.

When Agent Lacy met with Chief Bowles, he had riding with him John H. Reagan, Dr. W.G.W. Jowers and an interpreter named Cordra. Reagan was another young man who came to Texas as soon as he could from his home in Tennessee. He came to Texas as a nineteen-year old, and two years later, in 1839, he became a surveyor. Later he would be a U.S. Congressman from Texas, but at that time of his meeting with the Cherokee, he was a man who knew the "Lay of the land."

Agent Lacy found Chief Bowles to be hospitable as he seated them on a log near a spring that ran by his cabin. Instead of it being a polite visit, Lacy quickly accused the Cherokee of stealing, committing certain murders, and joining with Mexican rebels. He then changed directions by saying that he wanted the Cherokee to leave immediately and the government would pay them for the relocating move. Any improvements on the Cherokee land would not be considered. The Indians got nothing for their farms or houses. Basically, they were told to leave with a few clothes and provisions. Their homes would be confiscated by other settlers.

No wonder this decision was a big one for the Indians to make. As serious as the situation was, Chief Bowles was given only a week or ten days at the most to give Lacy his answer. When Lacy returned to the Indian camp, he saw a very sad Bowles. The Chief acknowledged that only he and one other council member wanted to leave. All the other leaders wanted to fight. In talking to Indian Agent Lacy, Bowles explained that he was 83-years old and would only live for a few more years. Bowles was worried about the welfare of his three wives and children. He explained, "If I fight, the whites will kill me. If I refuse to fight, my own people will kill me. I have led my people for a long time and I feel that it is my duty to stand by them regardless of what fate might befall me."

Their removal was discussed in "A Brief History of the Texas Cherokee" by Ira Kennedy. In this article, the plight of the Cherokee was mentioned as they began the long trek toward Mexico. They didn't get very far before the Texas Army intercepted them near Tyler on the Neches River. The army numbered about 500 troops, and the Cherokee tribe included 700 to 800 warriors, women, and children, but Bowles' warriors were routed. The fight went on for two days, first in Henderson County and then in Van Zandt. Chief Bowles' son John Bowles led the group of Cherokee southward because Chief Duwali Bowles was 83 years old at this time. The staff of leadership had changed hands.

Even though Chief Bowles wasn't the main leader, he carried his handsome sword and sash that Sam Houston had given him as he continued to ride his horse in the middle of the fight. (According to Utsidihi Hicks, a Cherokee historian, this sword is now located at the Masonic Lodge in Tahlequah, Oklahoma.) Most of the Indians lost their lives, and Chief Bowles was shot first in the leg. He got off his horse, set down with arms and legs crossed, and waited for death. The captain of the Texas militia, Robert W. Smith, walked up to Bowles and shot him in the head. Chief Bowles' mutilated body wasn't carried off the battle field. Instead, it was removed as strips of skin because the soldiers took a strip of skin from his body as a memento of the battle. One can't help but wonder, "Who was the real savage in this fight?" Today there is a monument commemorating his life, which is located near Alto, Texas, in Cherokee County. This battle occurred July 15, 16, 1839.

A few of the Cherokee people escaped this assault and finally slowed down their retreat several days later. John Bowles, Duwali's son, led the Cherokee in their retreat. When John managed to take his people to the Indian Territory, they weren't allowed to stay. John Bowles then decided to make a run for Mexico, hoping they could have a safe place away from the Texas army. After a long ride, they made it to West Texas. There they planned to rest a bit on the banks of the San Saba River. But they were attacked again by the Texas Rangers and Texas Army on Christmas Day, 1839. Many Cherokee were killed, including John Bowles. According to Cherokee historian Utsidihi Hicks, the soldiers stopped fighting when they discovered the tribe was Cherokee and provided food for the

Indians. The few Indians who survived fled quickly, and ended up in different places. Some went to Mexico, but many either went to Arkansas and Louisiana or sneaked back to their home in the piney woods of East Texas.

One small group of Cherokees stayed in Texas and lived on a river near Houston, Texas. They were quite industrious because they owned a ferry that they used to get people across the nearby river. This ferry was the type that men operated by using long poles to push the ferry across the river. Larry Anderson's great-granddad was a member of this group. According to the stories told by his family, these Cherokee were well thought of by the settlers in that area. When the soldiers came to their area looking for Indians in the 1850s, they left these particular Cherokee alone probably because the people living in the area needed the ferry.

Larry said that in this tribe, the women had quite a bit to say when important decisions were made. According to the family story, his great-grandmother was pretty strong willed. Sometimes her decisions were given dictatorially with no room for discussion. Larry said that when his great-granddad didn't agree with one of her decisions, he'd jump on his horse and ride away.

One other marker of significance has to do with the last big Cherokee battle in Texas involving Duwali Bowles. Chief Bowles had no funeral at the time of his death, so many years later the descendents of the tribe and friends decided to honor him. This event occurred 156 years later. On Sunday, July 16, 1995, they had a funeral service for Chief Bowles and the other tribe members who lost their lives in the battle. The funeral was held on the site of the Battle of Neches in Van Zandt County, Texas.

One other note of interest happened on November 25, 1997. At that time, the American Indian Heritage Center of Texas, Inc. purchased the land where the Battle of the Neches was fought in Van Zandt County near the community of Redland, Texas.

Even though some Cherokee kept good records of their ancestors, no one was able to reestablish the Texas Cherokee tribe for many years because to do so was illegal in Texas. But over the years, opinions slowly began to change. On August 14, 1993, a meeting was held in Troup, Texas to reorganize the Cherokee in Texas as a tribe. They have leaders and a constitution. One dream of the Cherokee Council is that eventually they will be able to buy enough land in Cherokee or Smith County to develop a living history museum and teaching facility.

Today the Cherokee Nation is very active with their offices in the W. W. Keeler Complex near Tahlequah, Oklahoma. This location is referred to as the capital of the Cherokee Nation. This organization has operated under a constitutional form of government since 1827, and enjoys more than 320,000 registered members scattered throughout the United States. The Cherokee improve their constitution each time a new one is created. In 2006, the Cherokee Nation voted and enacted their most recent version of their constitution, which calls for tri-partite governmental-judicial branches. According to their plans, their goal as a government is to help their citizens obtain a better quality of life, and education is an important factor of that dream.

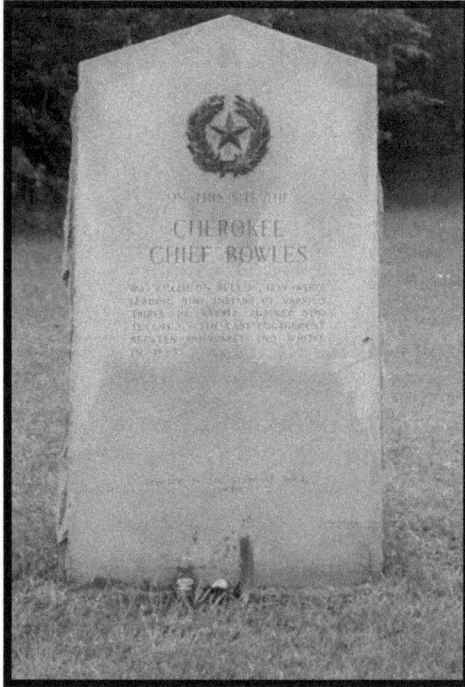

Chief Duwali Bowles' tombstone near the site of his last battle.

Ch. 3 The Tonkawa Tribe

If a white man visited a Tonkawa camp in the 1800s, they might be shocked to see an Indian eating a piece of human flesh and dancing the scalp dance with determined zeal. These hops and jumps continued way into the early morning hours or until they fell to the ground from exhaustion. Tonkawa were another tribe of Indians who left their mark, and the mark of their teeth, on early day Texans. They were known to be cannibals, but at the same time, the Tonkawa individuals reached out to the white man and to his religion as much as any tribe in Texas. In their early years, the Tonks consisted of many sub-tribes in eastern New Mexico, central Texas, and western Oklahoma. Their presence in Texas history suggests that they were here earlier than some of the better known tribes were. The Waco tribe called them by a name meaning "They all stay together," but the Tonkawa called their people "Tickanwa-tic," which meant "Real People."

Tonkawa migrated to Central Texas from the high plains as early as the 17th century. Each band was governed independently of the others up to this time. But the move to Texas changed their approach to government because several small bands were believed to have consolidated after t hey reached Tejas country. Women's lib advocates would have been excited about the government of Tonkawa tribes because another unusual trait of this group was their maternal clans, which were the basic unit in the Tonkawa society. Children became members of their mother's clan. So when a man took a wife, he lived with his spouse's clan. Tonkawa women were very strong of character, so they ruled their clan. Each clan saw themselves as a family unit, so they didn't encourage inter-marriage. The Tonkawa practiced levirate, which means a man was expected to marry his brother's widow. This practice of taking care of widows was mentioned in the Bible in Deuteronomy 25:5-10, but it isn't known whether the Bible had any influence on the Tonkawa during the 1700 and 1800s. In their culture, the same thing could happen where a sister would marry her dead sister's husband. Orphans became wards of the mother's clan.

The Texas Tonkawa Indians planted a few crops, but their main source of food was the buffalo and deer that they hunted. Tonkawa loved to move from one hunting ground to another, which was easy to do once they had horses. Having horses and some firearms to use along with their bow and arrows probably came as a result of them having a chance meeting with Spaniard explorers.

Tonkawa Indians. Courtesy of U. S. National Archives

If you gazed at one of these Indians, they didn't look much different than the other tribes. The Tonkawa dressed much like the Comanche but the men's breechclout was much longer than other tribes. Women wore a short skin skirt. Tonkawa males liked to paint and tattoo their bodies. They also enjoyed wearing earrings and necklaces, which were made from shells, bone, and feathers. Their moccasins were made of deer hide or of buffalo skin. Both male and female parted their hair in the middle of their head. The men wore their hair long or they braided it. But some of the women varied the accepted braids by cutting their hair short and unbraided. The women also wore tattoos. They painted black stripes on their mouths, noses and backs. Since the women wore little clothing except in the winter time, visitors would notice they had also painted concentric black rings on their breasts.

Tonkawa were hunters for the most part, so they enjoyed having deer or turkey to eat along with rabbits, skunks, rats, and land tortoises. They were known to eat rattlesnakes, which to them were a delicacy. The only animals they refused to consume were the wolves and coyotes because of their religious beliefs. These two animals were sacred to their tribe. Tonkawa liked fish and oysters and also gathered roots, fruit, and seeds. The red cactus fruit called tuna was also on their menu during the fall of the year.

Cabeza de Vaca may have been the first European to see the Tonkawa. If this statement is true, he would have crossed their trails between 1528 and 1536. This statement implies that the Tonkawa were in the Tejas country much earlier than some historians thought. Cabeza de Vaca traveled from the Texas coast near present-day Galveston with his companions for five years until he reached Mexico. When he described the Indians he met and the countryside through which he passed, it is possible that he saw the Tonks. This small group of travelers survived on the prickly pear fruit called tuna, and other edibles available. In Cabeza's writings, he doesn't mention the buffalo as a source of meat, but he does say that they saw some herds of the huge, shaggy beast two or three times. Rivers such as the Trinity, Brazos, Colorado, and the Rio Grande were crossed by de Vaca's group, but the route they used to accomplish this fete is uncertain.

It is assured that the Alonso de Leon's expedition in 1690 began a time of frequent contact between the Tonkawa and the Spanish in Texas. In 1721, the Marquis de Aquayo made a trip to Texas and studied the possibility of re-establishing missions that had been overtaken by the French. Father Pinella wrote a letter to the Parent College of Quere'tar, and his letter tells about this undertaking. The letter was preserved in the Spanish Archives. Marquis was an explorer who found himself caught in an unusual weather condition near the site of these future missions on the San Gabriel River. On November 21, 1721, he observed a tremendous ice storm, followed by snow. The weight of the precipitation pulled huge trees over so that their roots appeared out of the ground. Other trees had huge branches break off from the weight of the snow.

When the soldiers who were with Marquis counted the fallen trees in their camp, they discovered over two hundred pulled from the ground. They later recorded a total of over two thousand trees pulled from the ground in the outlying area. When the explorer returned from his trip, the priests listened to Marquis de Aquayo's report and seemed interested in having a mission there along the San Gabriel River.

But nothing happened in terms of mission building for a long time. Four Tonkawa chiefs wanted to know more about the message they had heard from a priest years before, so in 1744 these Tonkawa appeared at the mission in San Antonio and pleaded with the missionaries, "Come and tell us about your God." The interest that these Indian leaders showed was the actual reason that the missions were built. Well, really there was another reason: the Spaniards wanted to prevent the French and English from occupying the same area. They thought establishing missions would be a good way to prevent other countries from invading Texas. The friars got busy and planned to make three missions on the San Gabriel River in an area northeast of Austin near where the town of Rockdale is today.

The first mission, San Francisco Xavier de Horcasitas, was finished May 7, 1748. By 1749 the San Ildefonso and the Nuestra Senora De La Candelaria were complete also. Although the Tonkawa had asked for a mission, other tribes were involved with the missions such as the Mayeyes, Yerbipanes, Yojuanes, Orcoqiuisacs, Bifais, Cocos, and Deadoses.

The warring Apache didn't want to be Christianized, but they didn't like the presence of the missions either. In fact, the

Lipan Apache felt threatened by these men of God, so the missionaries decided they had better build a fort for protection. It seems like the fort wasn't to keep out anybody but the Apache. In 1751, Captain Felipe de Rabago Y Teran came to the missions with a group of soldiers, including a soldier named Juan Joseph Ceballos. The Captain Rabago was handsome and instantly fell in love with Ceballos' wife. The officer flirted with the lady, and infuriated her husband. When Ceballos couldn't stand the flirting anymore, he, told Rabago to leave his wife alone. Captain Rubago didn't care for Ceballos at all, so he had the man chained and beaten.

When Father Wan Jose Ganzabal told Captain Rabago to release Ceballos and stop bothering his wife, the Captain chained Ceballos to the wall and violated his wife in front of him. It was obvious the military, not the priests, were the men in charge. This atrocious behavior by the officer was too much for the Christian Fathers to take, so two priests rescued the prisoner and hid him in the church. But this action didn't stop the arrogant Captain. He rode his horse into the church, grabbed Ceballos and threw him in prison. The priests were so horrified that they had the Captain Rubago excommunicated from the church along with all of his men. But he continued to harass the missionaries. The priests had a lot more trouble with their military protectors than they did with the Apache Indians roaming around outside the fort.

Captain Rubago wouldn't let the priest's protection keep him from the man he wanted to exterminate, so at the first opportunity, Ceballos was killed, and most people thought the Captain should be returned to Spain to face his crimes. But the priests weren't strong enough to do anything about his atrocities, so he continued to rape the Indian women of the area, and this made the warriors madder than ever.

Because of the soldiers' actions, not the actions of the priests, this set of missions closed after being opened only ten years. The priests talked of moving somewhere farther west, and scouting commenced to find a good location. Because of the beautiful flowing San Saba River, the priests decided to move almost 180 miles westward to open a new mission there. But before they actually left the San Gabriel River region, strange weather hit the area. A ball of fire appeared in the sky. It was scary because it moved from the presidio toward the mission and back to the presidio. Then it exploded. The San Gabriel River stopped flowing, but other rivers and streams in the area were unchanged. An area of the land near the mission was called a plain, but it changed over the years to a thicket and huge, deep cracks appeared in the ground. A bad drought appeared only in the area where the missions had been. The area outside of this region had plenty rain. To say that Mother Nature didn't like the Mission was putting it lightly. Bizarre weather happened both before and after the San Gabriel Mission was constructed.

Captain Rabago was finally sent back to Spain to face an inquiry about his actions. Any priests who endured his behavior were probably happy when they heard he was bound for Spain. But later they found out that he wasn't punished, and to make this action more insulting, he returned to Texas to torment other people.

The Tonkawa Indians realized another reason why the missions failed. In these buildings beside the San Gabriel, the priests had hoped to Christianize the Tonkawa Indians, but what the Tonkawa actually saw happening was that their warriors had to protect the missionaries from other warlike tribes such as the Apache. Battles ensued between the two tribes. Although the Spanish had good intentions in their plan to help the Indians, the Tonkawa tribe finally decided life wasn't so good around these missions. While living there, they suffered several epidemics of disease such as small pox. The illnesses, plus the Apache raids, almost wiped out the Tonkawa. Since the Indians lost many tribe members, they pulled away from the missions, and this action also finalized the existence of the Spanish missionaries in that location. They closed the doors of their churches for good.

In 1755 the Spanish Friars made their next move in Texas to spread the Christian message, and they moved to a new location somewhat different then the old one in Central Texas where people were cultivating fields made lush with rainfall. The next location for a mission was many miles westward. In a strange series of circumstances, the Spanish missionaries moved southwest and built the Santa Cruz de San Saba Mission on the San Saba River about three miles east of modern day Menard, Texas. In 1755 there was not another human being in site at this location, only Indian raiding parties passed by from time to time.

Why the friars picked this spot for a mission has been a source of wonder for many historians. Of course, they hoped to reach the Apache who moved about in this area. Another reason for this undertaking was the support of a well-to-do man named Pedro Romero de Terreros. He was a wealthy mine owner who lived in Pachua. Romero agreed to finance the cost of building the mission and supplying it with twenty missionaries from Santa Cruz de Queretaro and San Fernando de Mexico for three years. He also stipulated that his cousin, Fray Alonso Giraldo de Terreros, would lead the enterprise. It could be said that Romero controlled this venture.

Presidio de San Luis de Amarillas' gate. Picture in author's Collection

47

Several events tied this new mission in with the old one that had been closed on the San Gabriel River. The new San Saba Presidio was built four miles upstream from the new mission, because it needed soldiers to protect the priests from harm. Col. Diego Ortiz Parrilla was appointed commander of this new presidio, so in September of 1756 he transferred fifty men from the defunct San Xavier garrison to the new presidio on the San Saba River. He collected other soldiers in San Antonio and in Mexico until he had enough to total 100 men. On April 6, 1857, soldiers, along with six missionaries and others totaling 300 people marched to the site on the San Saba River. With this number of soldiers, Col. Ortiz had the largest garrison in Texas, and it was called Presidio de San Luis de Amarillas. When it was completed, it was a pleasing structure with a rock arch over the entrance. It was built so that its outside walls were made of rock, and they protected the houses built inside for the soldiers. But the biggest problem for Ortiz was the fact that he was four miles from the mission he was supposed to protect.

This location for the San Saba Mission was very remote from any settlements, but its one advantage was flat land along the river that could be cultivated. The mission included a church and buildings to use as storage as well as cottages. Some people said the missionaries didn't want the worshippers to be influenced by the bad character of the soldiers, so they built the fort several miles from the mission. This decision would later haunt the church fathers because the fort was too far from the mission to protect it.

Almost immediately the priests tried to interest the Apache in religion at this location. At first the Indians seemed to like the missionaries, and they attended their services. Finally in June of 1857, the friars saw a huge number of Apache approaching their mission. The large group of Indians scared the missionaries, but they soon discovered that the 3,000 Apache were moving north to hunt buffalo. When the missionaries talked of worshipping God, the hunters weren't interested because they had buffalo on their mind. But before the Indians departed, they left two of their sick tribe members at the mission. They promised to come back after the hunt and worship with the priests.

As winter arrived, frigid weather enveloped the mission, and the cold winter killed the livestock that the missionaries had hoped to use as food. Then on February 25, 1758, Indians captured fifty-nine horses in the pasture nearby. All of this activity made Col. Ortiz at the presidio rather uneasy. Some of the early missionaries had left the mission during the year, so they had a small number of people trying to survive the winter in the remote mission. Ortiz urged the 36 people at the mission to come to the fort, but they refused. Nothing more was heard from the Indians for the next several months, so the priests were hopeful they could talk to the Indians and save their souls. As spring came to the San Saba River area, a few Indians stopped by the mission as they moved about in the warmer weather. As a friendly atmosphere seemed to exist, the Spanish Fathers relaxed.

But the mission had only been in business for about a year when the Comanche decided the Apache were getting special privileges at the mission. Even though the Apache came to the mission and listened to the missionaries, they never lived there. But the Comanche didn't know this, so they were jealous of the treatment the Apache were getting from the missionaries. They thought the Apache were receiving special gifts and food. Another Indian called El Mocho was also against this mission along the San Saba.

El Mocho had an interesting background. He was also called Tosche (left Hand.) As a small boy born into the Lipan Apache tribe, he was captured when the Tonkawa raided his village. He was eventually adopted into this tribe and showed shrewdness and leadership at an early age. When the Tonkawa migrated to West Texas, he noticed the new mission along the San Saba, and he was instrumental in suggesting to other chiefs that the Apache were getting too many favors from the priests.

Without warning, the Comanche suddenly turned on the mission and surrounded it March 15, 1758. The priests closed the gates, but they couldn't hold off their attackers. The Comanche attacked with arrows flying and fire blazing in the chapel. Soon all the buildings were burned and nearly all the people living there were killed. The soldiers were too far away from the mission to help at all. Only one friar, Father Miguel Molina, lived to tell about the burned mission. At this time the Tonkawa warriors, along with El Mocho, rode with the Comanche, so they aided in carrying the torches to burn this mission. The Spaniards had previously thought they had a peaceful relationship with the Tonkawa, but now they were leery of any Tonkawa tribe member because they saw them destroying the mission along with the Comanche.

In the fall of 1759, Col. Ortiz raised a force of about 600 men to fight the Comanche. He was still operating out of the San Saba Presidio upstream from the burned mission. He followed the Comanche to the Red River and attacked them near the modern day Fort Spanish. Ortiz was surprised at the strength of the Indians. After a few volleys of gunpowder, he had to retreat, and his loss was similar to other forces who tried to control the Indians. The warriors were competent foes because they had firearms from the French and horses from the Spanish. These two factors made the Comanche and other plains tribes a formidable foe for the next few decades.

Meanwhile the Tonkawa continued to move about the Texas frontier. El Mocho argued with the Tonkawa peace chief named Neques because Neques believed an alliance with the Spaniards would be good. But El Mocho was against the alliance because he wanted to drive the Spaniards as well as white settlers out of Texas. He was so against the missions that he continued to harass the missionaries until the last Apache mission was closed in 1769. During the 1770s, he continued to war against the Spaniards and the Apache. Finally the Spaniards agreed to pay the Tonkawa tribe for any scalps they might take of the Osage and the Apache tribe. El

Mocho made peace with the Spaniards only when he realized he would receive money.

The Tonkawa had enemies other than the missionaries. When the smallpox epidemic almost wiped out the tribe, most of the elders, as well as Chief Neques, lost their life. In that year, 1779, El Mocho was made the head chief of the Tonkawa. Surprisingly, after he was named chief, he wanted to celebrate with the Spanish leaders who lived in the village Taovayas on the Red River. While visiting them, he talked to the Spanish Indian agent named Athanase de Mezieres and promised him his loyalty and friendship. Mezieres thought he was serious, so he took El Mocho to visit the Spanish governor at Bexar. The Governor, Domingo Cabello y Robles, gave gifts to El Mocho and promised to give him help when needed.

But behind the Governor's back, El Mocho pressed all tribes to wipe out the Spaniards. The new Tonkawa chief went so far as to form an alliance for that purpose. He aligned himself with tribes such as the Lipan Apaches, the Comanches, with whom he had made peace in 1781; and the Caddoes. In January 1784, El Mocho led war parties against Spanish settlements. The Tonka were successful in these raids, and carried off captives along with stolen horses. The Spaniards had aligned with other tribes who tried to stop El Mocho, but the Tonkawa defeated them. El Mocho often needed more horses, so in 1782, he traded guns to Lipan warriors for horses. Now he was ready to go on another raid.

El Mocho was so powerful with his influence on the Tonkawa tribe, as well as other groups, that the Spaniards plotted to have him killed. It was surprising how the Tonkawa had at one time been friendly with the Spaniards but under El Mocho's leadership they were encouraged to turn against their Spanish friends. Those old "friends" felt that El Mocho was too powerful for his own good. After two attempts to assassinate El Mocho, the Spaniards finally succeeded in 1784. In July of 1784, El Mocho was invited to a conference at the presidio at La Bahia. At that meeting, he was assassinated. After this event, the Tonkawa were friendlier with the Spanish than they had been while under El Mocho's leadership.

By the 1800s, the Tonkawa were looking for alliances. Besides getting along with the Lipan Apache, the Tonkawa also became friendly with the Texans who came pouring into that state. As this new situation emerged, the Tonkawa were preparing to soon elect a new Head Chief. Their thoughts turned to one of their own highly respected warriors. Tonkawa Chief Placido, called Ha-shu-la-na, was born in Texas in 1788. Placido, which meant "Can't kill him," in Tonkawa, was the son of a Tonkawa chief and a Comanche mother who had been captured as a young person. In an interesting turn of events, she went from being the tribe's slave to being the chief's wife.

Chief Placido of the Tonkawa. Courtesy of Texas State Library and Archives Commission

Placido grew into manhood and walked the trail of leadership like his father. Chief Carita was the head chief of their Tonkawa tribe while Placido was becoming a man, but Carita died in 1823. At this point, Placido was selected Head Chief.

The first white man that Placido helped was James Long who made the Long Expedition to Texas in 1819. James Long was a doctor and a merchant who lived in Natchez, Mississippi. He was displeased with the recent treaty, the Adams-Onis Treaty, which traded Florida to the United States and released Texas to Mexico. He couldn't believe that the United States would make such a swap, so he recruited some soldiers to help him go to Texas and get that territory back. James Long gathered 300 men by subscription to travel with him. They were promised they would receive land in Texas if they would help him capture Texas from the Mexican rule and set up a Republic of their own. Long's men had their first taste of battle when they fought the Mexican Army in Nacogdoches in the fall of 1821. Long's men defeated the Mexican Army, and Chief Placido and his Tonkawa warriors were part of this victory. For their help, he and his men received horses and scalps.

Long set up a Republic of Texas government at the site of his first triumph. Feeling successful, he decided to venture further by attacking the Mexicans at the Presidio LaBahia. One look at that monstrous structure on the San Antonio River should have changed his mind. It looked like a medieval castle with its tall stone walls. This fortress had been located there since 1770. When he attacked the Presidio LaBahia, Long's men won and then entered the Presidio. They enjoyed three days of life in the fortress before the Mexican army retaliated and beat them soundly. Several officers including Long were captured. James Long with other Texans was taken on the long road to Mexico. While in captivity, a guard accidently shot and killed James Long. Some people think the guard may have been given money to kill this man.

There are no details as to what happened to the Tonkawa scouts after this battle, but Chief Placido lived to fight another day. He waited until some other Texas leader needed a scout and that time eventually came when the Comanche were giving everybody trouble. When Stephen F. Austin was trying to bring settlers into Texas in the 1820s, the Comanche were his biggest threat. Austin tried to fulfill a dream that his Daddy, Moses Austin, had where many new families would become a part of Texas.

After Moses died, Stephen F. Austin knew he had to get the right to settle families in Texas by going to Mexico. Although Austin was born in Virginia, he had lived for a number of years in Missouri. That area was governed by the Mexican government, so he was acquainted with Mexicans and knew how to do business with them. He traveled to Mexico City to obtain permission to bring 300 families into the Texas area. When he arrived at the office that handled grants, he was probably surprised to see other people talking to the Mexican government about getting land in Texas. One of the men he saw when he was in Mexico was Cherokee Chief Bowles. (See Ch.1 about Chief Bowle's experience.)

The Tonkawa Indians sided with Austin and in 1824 he had Chief Placido and thirteen other Tonk scouts working for him as they fought against the Comanche. This convenient alliance with the white leader probably came about because the Tonkawa had been battling the Spanish on and off for years in Texas. They saw a chance to line up with the new Texans and get away from the Comanche and Spaniards. From this time forward, the Comanche, as well as other tribes, had little use for the Tonks, as they were called. While Placido was helping Austin, he lived near the springs in the San Marcos River. He and his men helped the white man fight other tribes in the area such as the Caddo, Wichita, and the Waco.

When the state officially organized the Texas Rangers in November of 1835, you know who was nearby ready to enroll? Chief Placido quickly joined the Texas Rangers and encouraged his warriors to do the same. The Tonkawa scouts were with the Texans fighting the Comanche August 12, 1840 at Plum Creek. (See more of this battle in Chapter 5) Placido was also in the battle a few days later at Linnville. Some observers of the battle noticed the Tonkawa jogged on foot some of the time while their Ranger friends rode horseback. One story about the Tonkawa relates how Chief Placido and his men placed their hands on the rump of a Ranger's horse and jogged 30 miles while the Rangers sat in the saddle and rode their horses in the same direction. Since the warriors were successful in that particular battle, the Rangers told them to each select a horse from the Comanche's ponies that were milling about. At least, the Tonkawa got to ride in style on their way home.

Chief Placido had a long career as a scout because in1846, he was scouting with the mixed blood Cherokee Bill Chisholm and leading Jack Hays and his Texas Rangers into battle against some Comanche in West Texas. Hayes had scouting reports that the Comanche were headed to the sacred spot on the Concho River where Indians had left drawings for many years. (This location is about 30 miles east of the present day town of San Angelo.) Although Hays had failed in a past Comanche encounter, he meant to surprise them this time. He and his Rangers beat the Indians to the Painted Rocks on the Concho River and waited for their arrival.

As the Rangers walked along the river, they saw a bluff that was a short distance from the river. They noticed pictographs on the limestone bluff parallel to the river. These paintings were drawn at different times and many of the sketches told a story. Colors of red, orange, yellow, and black described hunting expeditions with drawings of buffalo and deer. The Rangers saw other drawings that looked like the Mission San Saba. These drawings on a 70 feet tall limestone cliff dated back from 1300 to 1650, the Toyah Period. As the Rangers waited quietly for the Indians, they probably felt the spirits of warriors of the past as well as the spirits of the ones they expected to attack when they crossed the Concho River in a little while. The Comanche had no idea of the surprise attack waiting for them. They rode straight into an ambush.

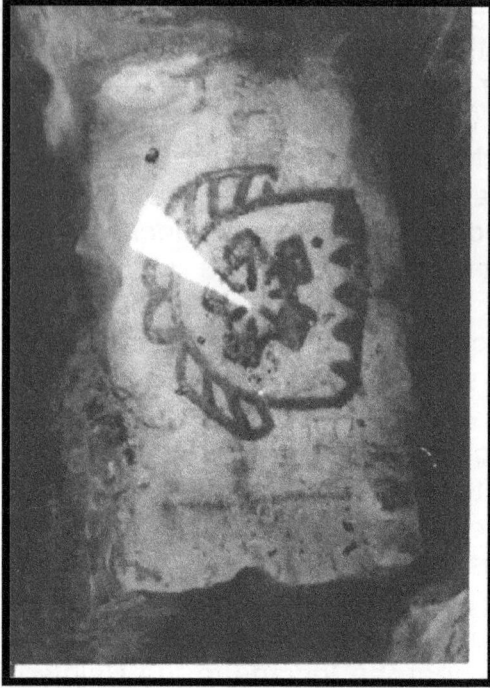

The bright light is the sun shining on solstice day, December 22 at the Painted Rocks. The theory is that many years ago several tribes may have met at the Painted Rocks on that day to join in rituals to celebrate. Courtesy of the Fred Campbells, owner of the Painted Rocks site.

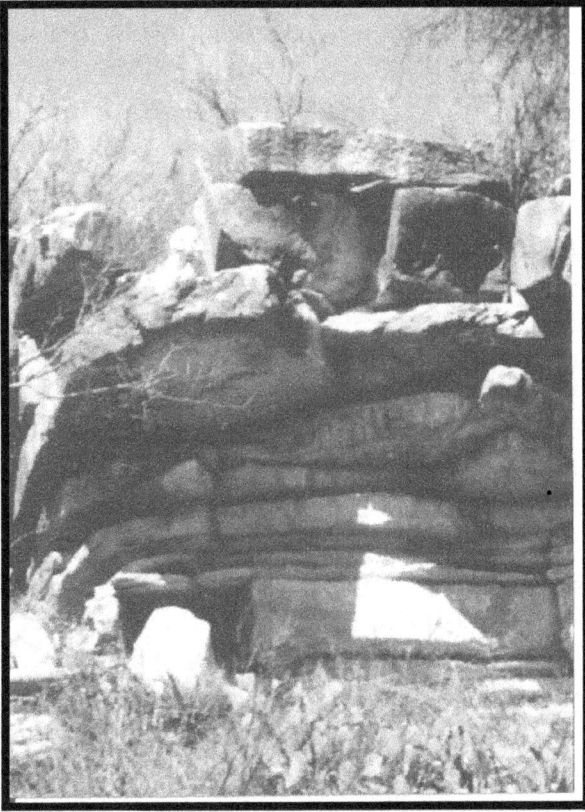

The Painted Rocks are on a cliff near the Concho River, Author's Collection

The Rangers attacked with a volley of rifle shots coming from an ambush. The battle raged for some time but Hays won this one. The Comanche were totally rioted. Jack Hays had to give his scouts a lot of credit for the successful battle. Wayne R. Austerman in "Ambush and Siege at Paint Rock," told what one Ranger said about the Tonkawa scouts, "They could trail them Comanche like a dog-eared hound" and "would put their head down and look like they were smelling their tracks." It was well known that Chief Placido hated the Comanche, and they detested him because of his cannibalistic traits.

The other scout, Cherokee Bill Chisholm was the son of Jesse Chisholm the well-known Cherokee who gave his name to the Chisholm Trail as he sent his cattle to market. Since the older Jesse was known as a guide and trailblazer, some of his knowledge must have spilled over on his offspring.

Even though Tonkawa warriors helped Jack Hays and should have been in good graces with the Texans, something happened in 1848 that put Chief Placido on the run from the law. When Texas was annexed by the United States in 1846, a floodgate was opened for settlers to come to the Lone Star state. White settlers entering the new land were known to hunt and kill game on Tonkawa land. As hard as Placido tried to control his warriors, he failed when they attacked some settlers. Two white men were killed near Fredericksburg, and eventually two Tonkawa warriors admitted to Placido that they killed the men and ran away before they were caught. Chief Placido was often around the white men's towns, and became afraid the law would apprehend him for the crimes of two of his tribesmen. Thinking absence might be good, Chief Placido left the country for awhile. When he returned some time later, the deaths were old news and no Tonkawa was ever tried for the deaths of the two settlers.

The earlier days of Tonkawa history are hard to recover for sure. In the 1700s a group of independent Indian bands such as the Mayeyes, Cava, Cantona, Emet, Sana, Toho and Tohaha grouped together with the Tonkawa to form a tribe in Central Texas. According to history, the Tonkawa were a small band themselves who were seeking allies. The Waco meaning of Tonkawa was "they all stay together," and that's what these small groups decided to do, probably for protection from larger tribes.

The Tonkawas had different dances to commemorate different parts of their lives. On the website "Tonkawa Tribal Ceremonials" the tribe explained how they celebrated their "origin of life" dance with the solemn "Wolf Dance." Since the subject of the dance was very special, they tried to keep it a secret from non-tribe members. Their "Water Drum" dance has religious significance and is called the "Peyote Ritual" where peyote is used s a sacrificial medicine. This particular worshipful dance dates back to before Columbus' discovery of America. Some of the Spanish and French explorers remember hearing about this dance in the 1600s. In recent years, this "sacrificial medicine" has been adapted to the Tonkawa's religious ceremonies. Outsiders have named this ceremony the "Native American Church," but the Tonkawa and Lipan Indians know that this ceremony is as old as the origin of their people.

Even though the Tonkawa had a proud heritage, the tribe in the 1800s depended largely on the United States government for survival. As the Tonkawa tribe decreased in size, the soldiers at the Texas forts noticed them living near their garrisons. The Tonks had their homes within running distance to the fort. It wasn't long before even more soldiers galloped their horses through the tall grass on the plains of Texas. Their arrival came about because more settlers were attacked by the aggressive Comanche and Apache. Finally the United States government heard their plea. Platoons of soldiers now graced the prairie. Probably the travel of one important soldier made an impact too.

Army Captain Randolph B. Marcy took a trip through Texas because the government wanted him to map out a military route from Fort Smith in Arkansas to Santa Fe, New Mexico. Marcy led a group of California immigrants on this trip in 1849. On the way back, he crossed the Clear Fork of the Brazos near the future site of Fort Griffin. Marcy mentioned in his military communications that he felt that Texas needed more protection, so his recommendations led to the creation of Fort Belknap about 80 miles southwest of Fort Worth and Fort Phantom Hill north of present Abilene. These forts were started in 1851 and Fort Chadbourne was created on a tributary of the Colorado River a year later. These forts would eventually be a part of the Tonkawa's life.

More white settlers pushed northwest in Texas searching for land. The Indian tribes in that area were in the white man's way. White settlers wanted the good land that was a part of the Indian Reservation, so they accused the Indians of cattle thievery that was probably done by white men dressed like Indians. The tension got so bad by the 1850s, the Tonkawa were one of several tribes who were selected to be placed on a reservation in Young County. During this time, the Tonkawa, along with other tribes, suffered greatly from white Texans who repeatedly attacked the Reservation Indians. Finally Indian Agent Richard Neighbors moved the Tonkawa to a reservation in Oklahoma where he thought they would be safe.

But some of the Tonkawa continued to be scouts for the government. In 1858 the Rangers fought Comanche on the Canadian River Campaign. Chief Placido served under Shapley Ross in this battle because Ford's Rangers and the Brazos Reservation Rangers both were involved. Years later when Rip Ford wrote his memoirs, he said, "The Indian allies behaved most excellently on the field of battle. They deserve well of Texans and are entitled to the gratitude of the frontier people." Chief Placido stayed involved with the Rangers for many years, and he encouraged his men to enlist also. The sad thing is that they served for little or no pay.

These Tonkawa were the same Indians who had been considered valuable scouts and warriors when they helped the Texas Rangers and the army. Chief Placido died around 1862, but Johnson was the name of the chief Tonkawa scout who served under Ranald Mackenzie. Johnson helped the troops when they chased the Comanche across the Staked Plain. They did see some Comanche warriors from a distance when they traveled all the way into New Mexico in 1872, but no shots were fired.

Mackenzie made another attempt at corralling the Comanche when he and his troops located them in the Palo Duro Canyon in 1874. Ranald Mackenzie had about 20 Tonkawa scouts with him plus one captured Comanche on this trip. September 28, 1874, Mackenzie slipped into the Canyon.

Chief Johnson, Tonkawa scout for Ranald Mackenzie.

This is the same scene where Black Seminole scouts performed so well. Now the Tonkawa were also a part of this story and their part of the Army's success is to be unfolded.

The soldiers, along with scouts, made it to the floor of the Palo Duro before the Indians saw them. Most of the Comanche ran for their lives and scaled the Canyon walls successfully. What they left behind is the tragic part of the story. The Comanche left their teepees, buffalo robes, food and equipment that would fortify them through the coming winter.

Mackenzie let the Tonkawa scouts loot the Comanche camp and grab what they wanted. Some 1,500 Comanche horses were also left in the floor of the canyon. The soldiers didn't want to drive that many horses back to the fort, so Mackenzie had to make a decision about what to do with them. After soldiers and scouts picked some horses from the herd to keep, the soldiers were ordered to destroy the rest. This mass killing of horses sealed the fate of many Comanche. They froze or starved to death in the coming months.

Even though Tonkawa scout Johnson and his men served well when riding with soldiers such as Mackenzie, they were part of the tribe that white settlers detested. Every time a cow was missing or trouble appeared, the Tonkawa were blamed. The Tonkawa were probably innocent of most of the charges brought against them, but when the time came for placement of the Indian tribes, they were herded to the Indian Territory of Oklahoma like all the other Texas Indians.

The 2nd Cavalry's Major George Thomas led the army escort that took them to the Indian Territory. The Tonkawa may have been forced to leave their home by some of the same soldiers they had fought beside just a short time before. Just as the Cherokee were sent on their "trail of tears" without proper protection from the cold, the Tonkawa were asked to depart without most off their possessions.

Indian Agent Neighbors knew these Indians and had an emotional tie to the mistreated tribe. He was very sad to leave them in this new land. Some of his friends said they could see tears in his eyes when he left the almost defenseless Tonkawa in Oklahoma.

After the Tonkawa were moved to Oklahoma, they had to live side-by-side with other tribes who disliked them. The small number of Tonkawa men and women were attacked by some of the Delawares, Shawnees, Wichitas, and Caddos who lived on the reservation. Indians were fighting Indians. In 1862 these aggressive tribes almost snuffed out the Tonkawas. Of the 300 Tonkawas who were displaced in Oklahoma at that time, 137 of their tribe were killed. Chief Placido was also killed, but his son, Charlie survived. Charlie took the last of the tribe with him to Texas so they could live near Fort Griffin for protection. They stayed there until the end of the Civil War.

In the late 1870s, the Tonkawa lived in the area of the military Fort Griffin and the town by the same name. The fort was on hill and therefore elevated from the town situated in the flat land below. It was a thriving town at that time with cattle herds passing through as they followed the Western Trail on the way to Kansas and buffalo hunters buying supplies in the mercantile stores. At the towns' highest population count, Fort Griffin had 1,000 permanent residents who could read their newspaper, the Fort Griffin *Echo*. Visitors could come to town by way of the Butterfield Stage, which ran near town where the stage horses splashed in the river at the Clear Fork Crossing and deposited the stage's occupants.

With so many transient people passing through town, many undesirables visited the stores and saloons of Fort Griffin. Beautiful Lottie Deno, always clothed in the latest style of dress, was a successful gambler who showed up every time the soldiers had pay day. She found herself in the same poker game as Doc Holiday and Wyatt Earp. Outlaws like John Wesley Hardin, and John Selman walked the streets of Fort Griffin, so the Tonkawa had plenty chances to see the Sheriff in action.

The Tonkawa felt at home in this area, even though they didn't get involved in many of the town's activities. Ordinarily the Indians caused no trouble around the community, but every now and then they got hold of some whiskey. Then the Tonkawas livened things up along Main Street because it was full of half-drunk Indians. On August 23, 1879, the Indians got drunk, were very noisy, and didn't settle down when darkness arrived. Instead, they began to fight each other. When Constable Walker strolled toward the noise, the drunk Indians headed to the bushes. Walker apprehended seven of them and put them in his jail. Wails and cries of the jailbirds were heard all over the area that night, but the next morning, all was tranquil along the streets because the Tonkawas were sober. According to a newspaper account of the incident in the *Echo,* Constable Walker gave each inmate "a kick and a cuff" before he set them free.

After the Civil War, Governor J.W. Throckmorton asked the Texas legislature to donate a league of land to the Tonkawa, as well as supplies. Most of the tribe settled in that area and continued scouting for the army until Fort Griffin was closed in 1881. In March of 1881, the last 115 remaining Tonkawa had left the fort and camped in Joe Matthew's pasture about six miles from town. They had nowhere else to go and Mr. Matthews was a kind person. Some people in the town of Fort Griffin cared for the destitute Indians so they circulated a report to the Texas Legislature that stated the needs of the Tonkawa tribe.

This letter asked that the State of Texas provide a 3,000 acre plot for the tribe. They also felt that $10,000 was needed to help the Indians fence in their land, build their homes, buy farm implements, and furnish them with food and clothing for the next two years. At that time, the editor of the article felt that the Tonkawas could be self-sustaining. He finished the write-up by saying, "There is no tribe of Indians that have just claims upon the people as the Tonks, and they have received less than all others. It is hoped that the legislature will take hold of this matter promptly and relieve these unfortunate creatures."

According to "Tonkawa Tribal History" on their official website, their tribe members were allowed to stay in Texas until 1884. At that time, they were removed from Fort Griffin in October of 1884 and taken to a railroad station in Cisco, Texas. There the Tonkawa were placed on railroad cars and shipped to Sac-Fox Agency near Stroud, Oklahoma. An Indian child born on this trip was called "Railroad Cisco." When springtime came around, the tribe was loaded in wagons and sent 100 miles to the Ponca Agency. Spring rains had swelled the rivers, so the wagons had slow-going in deep mud. On June 30, 1885, the travelers reached their final destination, Oakland. As many Tonkawa look back at this incident, they think of it as a very sad time. It was such a significant event in their history that the modern day Tonkawa Tribe has their annual Pow-Wow on the last weekend of June to honor this sad time in tribal history.

People who lived near the Tonkawa had their memories of the tribe. John H. Jenkins was a settler in the Bastrop area. He said that the Tonkawa he noticed were much smaller and slenderer than the Comanche. One time a Tonkawa captive ran a foot race with a Comanche and beat him easily, according to Jenkins.

Texas Ranger, Noah Smithwick, said that once the Tonkawa moved near the white people, they were very interested in the social affairs that took place in the white settlements. In Smithwick's book, *The Evolution of a State,* he said it didn't matter whether the Indians were invited or not. The Tonkawa showed up at dances and outdoor religious services. They killed deer, and if they had more than they needed for their family, they sold the meat to the trading post. Since the Tonkawa lived near the white settlements, traders knew them well. One day a white man asked a Tonkawa hunter why he didn't kill turkey and sell them like he did the deer.

The Tonk had a surprising answer when he explained, "Oh, turkey too hard to kill. Injun crawl along in the grass, deer; he say 'Maybe so, Injun; maybe so stump,' and then he go on eat. Injun crawl a little closer and shoot him. Turkey look, 'Injun, by God,' and he duck his head and run."

The Tonkawa loved to gather pecans when they became edible in the fall. They scampered about under the trees and picked up as many as they could find in their area. The delicious meat of this nut could be eaten or it could be sold at the local trading post. The Indians didn't seem to notice whether they were picking up pecans that belonged to somebody's orchard or not. Several times the orchard owners got mad at the Indians for stealing their crop, so they fired a warning volley a time or two because the Indians were cutting off the big branches from the pecan trees before they picked the pecans. The Tonks thought they were speeding up the process, but they were actually killing the goose that laid the golden egg. Chief Placido saved the day by interceding and keeping everybody calm. Placido said, "I never shed the white man's blood."

So the question comes up as to why they were disliked by fellow Indians. As early as the eighteenth-century, Spanish explorers reported that the Tonkawa were "disliked and even abhorred" by other Indians. Captain Randolph Marcy related that they were "renegades and aliens from all social intercourse with other tribes."

Even Captain John Ford, leader of the Texas Rangers, who had seen just about every weird creature in Texas called them "black beasts."

Cannibalism was one trait that set the Tonkawa apart from most of the tribes. Several reliable accounts say that Tonkawa were known to have a ceremony where they ate portions of their dead enemies. Most people believed this ceremony was tied into their religion. Because of this horrible characteristic, other Indians would kill the Tonkawa when they had a chance. Everybody seemed to be against them, and the Tonkawa were against everybody.

When the buffalo became scarce, the Tonkawa no longer had beautiful hides to cover their teepees as in days past. Instead, they covered their lodge poles with whatever they found such as brush, grass, and branches. As they became poorer and fewer in number, Tonks used a brush arbor much like white men made when they built a temporary structure. Their poverty and small numbers caused them to side with the military for survival. As a result of this dependence, they became some of the best guides the U. S. Army had.

Even though the army shuffled them off to Oklahoma, the Tonkawa now call that state their home. I visited with Don Patterson May 29, 2013 over the phone. Dan is currently president of the Tonkawa Tribe of Oklahoma. He said that most of the tribe lives in Fort Oakland near the small town of Tonkawa, Oklahoma. Don said, "We have about 100 houses in this complex." Although there are about 665 Tonkawa people living in that complex, he said some Tonkawa live a few miles from Oakland. The location of Oakland is 100 miles north of Oklahoma City. Dan said the area is covered with wheat farms. The Tonkawa Tribe operates a casino in that area, and Dan says that it helps the tribe financially, but he also said, "We are struggling to survive."

Texans around San Marcos remember the story about Chief Placido helping the Rangers and the Texas soldiers fight the Comanche tribes, so the area could be settled. He is considered a legend in this area, so the community erected a monument to him in 2007. Chief Placido's statute is situated in the City Park of San Marcos near the San Marcos River where he lived. The monument is to celebrate how he helped the settlers establish San Marcos.

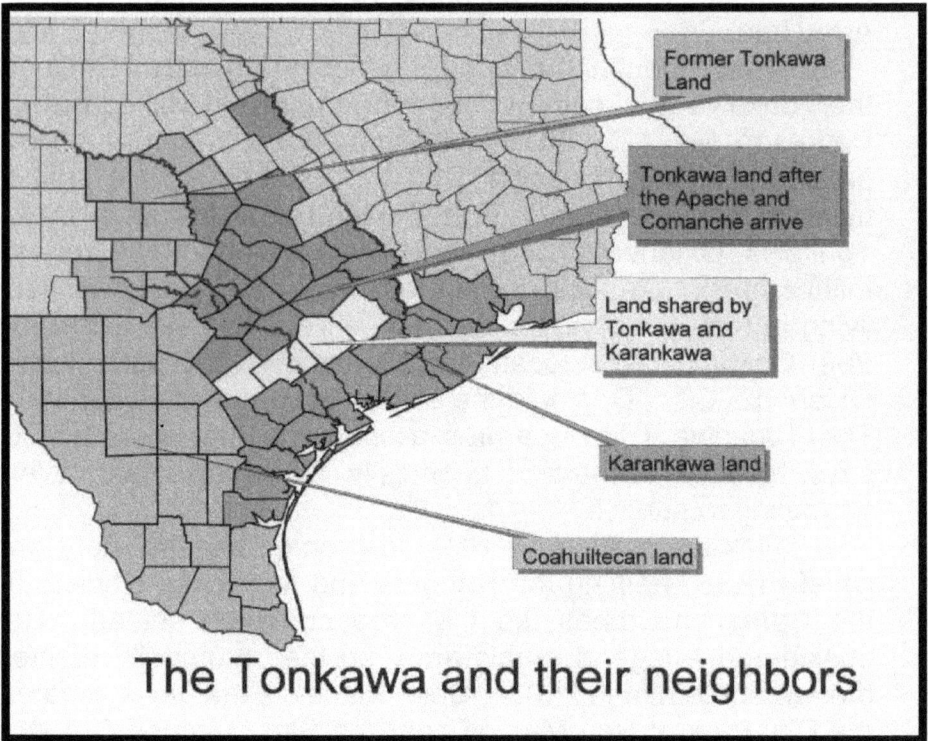

The Tonkawa and their neighbors

Tonkawa Map. Courtesy of U. S. National Archives

Ch. 4 Jumano Indians

A study of Jumanos should be called "The Study of the Lost Tribe." But when you take a guess at which tribe came first to Texas, you might be surprised that the Jumanos were historically one of the very earliest Indian groups living in Texas. They were thought to be there in the year 1000 or earlier. Whereas most tribes stayed in the general area of other tribes of the same name, the Jumanos bands were several hundred miles apart from each other and were scattered all over Texas. It wasn't unusual for these groups to live 200 miles apart. So when the Spaniards met these small Indian bands, they named them names like the Wichita (Taovaya) who lived in eastern New Mexico and some in Arizona. These visitors from Spain also called the Jumano such names as Xumana, Jumana, Humana, Umana, Xoman, or Sumana. This mix up made it more difficult for historians in later years to figure out which name went with which tribe.

According to Nancy P. Hickerson in *The Humanos: Hunters and Traders of the South* Plains, the Jumano Indians could have included three distinct groups: the Pueblo Indians near Salinas, New Mexico, which was about 40 miles south of Albuquerque; another group along the Rio Grande and Rio Conchos in Mexico; and a third group who were Caddo speaking Wichitas who lived along the Arkansas and Red Rivers. But it is now known that another group of Jumanos lived along the Concho Rivers in West Texas, a site where the rivers came together at the location of present-day San Angelo, Texas, and this group of Jumanos caused quite a stir when they urged priests to come to their tribe and baptize them. So little was known about the Jumanos that the Catholic leaders didn't know they existed, so they didn't respond to their need for a priest right away.

Although their history is very hard to locate, when the Spanish explorers visited their region, the Jumano tribes treated their visitors with reverent hospitality. In fact, the Indians were so kind, that their behavior made a great impression on the men riding horses and covered with their heavy armor. Spanish explorers gave us some insight into the Jumanos because they met them before many other settlers did. Explorers such as Alvar Nunez Cabeza DeVaca traveled through Jumano land in 1535 but he didn't record the names of the tribes. At the time he found the Jumano village, they lived in La Junta along the Rio Grande. Cabeza de Vaca only referred to them as the "People of the cows."

How this Spaniard found the Jumanos is quite a story. Cabeza de Vaca and other Spaniards arrived in America with five ships, and most of his 600 men who had started the journey. Five Franciscan friars also accompanied the voyage. The group was called the Panfilo de Narvaez Expedition. The ships located land that the explorers and the Spaniards thought was Mexico. But what they really discovered was the coast of Florida. Thinking they were close to their destination, De Vaca and a large group of men headed overland to find Mexico. Although they stayed near the seashore, so they could watch for the Spanish boats, they never saw the Spanish fleet again.

By this time the land explorers had nearly starved to death in this new world, so they had eaten all forty of their horses. After realizing they would have to manage for themselves, De Vaca helped his group make simple boats so they could sail to Mexico themselves. They made five boats from nearby material at the water's edge and pitched the holes with resin from the pine trees. They used the mane and tails from their horse carcasses to make rigging for the boats. In August of 1528, they used their clothes to make crude sails, so they were on their way to Mexico with pretty good homemade boats, but they had little covering on their bodies.

By September these unique sailors slipped away from the coast and sailed the high seas. A little bit of corn they had found along the way made up their total food for the voyage. When the surviving men jumped out of their two boats and waded ashore in November, they were on Texas soil, not Mexican as they supposed, and very lost.

Cabeza de Vaca related in his journals that he and his men nearly froze to death that December because they had no clothes. They built a fire on the shore to keep warm, but they also had visitors. Some very tall Indians who were probably the Karankawas appeared on the shore. The Spaniards were given food and allowed to live with this tribe. Cabeza de Vaca recorded the behavior of this tribe during the next several years.

The Karankawa were very athletic. They lived off of the food they found in the ocean and plant life, so they moved very often. Mosquitoes were a big problem in that coastal region, so they plastered their bodies with shark grease to survive the pesky insects. Years later, the Spaniards found out that the Karankawa were cannibalistic, especially if they had killed an enemy. But Cabeza de Vaca didn't mention ever seeing any evidence of this. Life in the humid coastal area was hard on the sailors from Spain. By 1832, nearly all the Spaniards were dead. A few of the survivors decided to stay with the Indians, but Cabeza de Vaca wanted to find Mexico. He had three friends who wanted to travel with him to Mexico by going overland. A Negro named Estavanico went with him as well as captains Andres Dorantes and Alonso del Casatilla.

The red fruit on prickly pear cactus were tasty. The Indians showed Cabeza de Vaca how to eat the fruit called tuna. Author's collection.

The four men headed west and no one knows their actual route for sure. They walked through a lot of cactus and mesquite and got their bodies torn even more. The Texas Indians they met on their travel proved to be helpful. They were friendly and showed them how to eat the fruit of the prickly pear called the tuna. These southwestern delicacies were a purplish-red fruit covered with tiny stickers. If a person could burn off the stickers, they could have a delicious meal. Cabeza was thought by some Indians to be a healer, so he was forced to look at the sick Indians who came his way along the trip. Some of the sick ones lived after he prayed for them, so the Indians were gracious in giving the explorers venison and tuna to eat.

When the travelers left the villages and lost their sense of direction, two Indian women came to their aid. These squaws served as guides and found food for them to eat. Remember at this point, Cabeza de Vaca and his crew had little clothing and no firearms to help defend themselves. The food given to them by the Indian women was greatly appreciated. The explorers were quoted as saying, "This was the thing on earth that made us most happy and for it we gave infinite thanks to our Lord."

The Spaniards found the Jumanos at La Junta along the Rio Grande. When they came to their camp, they saw a village consisting of hundreds of huts. LaJunta was located west of the present-day Big Bend area and was a term used to describe the fertile land where Rio Conchos River brought a large amount of water out of northern Mexico and dumped it into the Rio Grande. From this point of the rivers flowing together, the Spaniards came to a Jumano village in this area. When the four travelers came to the village, not a single Indian came out of their house, according to W. W. Newcomb in *The Indians of Texas*. This action surprised the Spaniards. When these first explorers looked inside the homes, the Indians were seated with their heads down and faces to the wall. Although this behavior was surprising, de Vaca later understood its meaning. The Indians didn't know if the explorers would stay with them in their village, but the Jumanos were giving the explorers great respect because they thought they were Gods. The Jumanos gave gifts to the Spaniards and acted as if they liked them.

Cabeza de Vaca and his men probably dined well while visiting these Indians. They had fish and mollusks from the river, and when in season, they gathered pecans to eat. The Jumanos also hunted deer and buffalo for meat and hides.

After the visitors got to know the Jumano better, the Spaniards seemed to need help, so the friendly Indians escorted them farther on their journey. The normal trade route for the Jumanos was northwestward over the Pecos River at Horsehead Crossing. They walked with the Spaniards into New Mexico.

Only when the Espejo Expedition of 1582-83 moved across Texas many years later did the Spanish give names to the Jumano tribe. Antonio de Espejo was an interesting man to be exploring Texas and searching for a missing priest named Father Rodriquez. It was a well-known fact that Espejo was a fugitive from a murder charge, so he needed to hide in an area where nobody knew him. The wastelands of Texas were a good hiding place for him because he could travel about the Indian tribes with no fear of identity. When Espejo and his men found the Jumano, they had changed their opinion of the Spaniard explorer from their first concept in 1535. No longer did the Jumanos think the Spanish were Gods, so they didn't bow to them on their second journey. Now the Spanish mentioned the tribe in their records and stated that instead of being afraid, the tribe now acted very friendly. The Spaniards met a hunting group of Jumanos between the Pecos River and LaJunta. This location is in the far southwestern part of Texas. Later they visited the Jumano village and said there were two hundred men and women singing to them as they rode up to their pueblo-styled homes. The Jumano gave the Spaniards gifts of deerskin clothing, colored feathers, and mescal. These natives were a gentle, pleasant Indian.

Along the Rio Grande near modern-day Redford, Texas, Jumanos built permanent homes similar to pueblos. Redford was southeast of the La Junta area located in what we now call the Big Bend. Some of these homes seen by explorers reminded them of the multifamily structures they saw elsewhere in the southwest, but homes in some Jumano communities weren't connected together like the ones in the pueblos. Each home was separate from the others. W.W. Newcomb in *The Indians of Texas* describes these homes as being twenty-eight by thirty feet in size. Luxan, who traveled with de Vaca, said half the house was built in a pit. Probably this maneuver was for insulation. The Jumano builders made houses of "turtle-back shaped bricks sitting longitudinally and plastered together." Their roofs were made of brush and branches covered with a coating of adobe.

The Jumano story of prominence existed before the Spanish or other aggressive Indian tribes entered Texas and before climate changes took place that altered their way of living. Since we now know that the Jumano bands had homes both on the Rio Grande in Texas and the Rio Grande northward into New Mexico, the question comes as to whether these groups of Indians were slightly different Indians. This tribe was also found in other parts of Texas such as the Concho Rivers near present-day San Angelo and in the Panhandle, but many questions about them remain unanswered.

Although the Spaniards used this name to also describe Indians in New Mexico and in Arizona, the name "Jumano" seems to identify a tribe of Indians who painted or tattooed their body. They made circles around their arms and body parts. These Indians were attractive and had a pleasant personality according to Spaniards who met them. The name "Jumano" was used by both gardeners who had pueblos along the Rio Grande and by hunters who roamed various parts of Texas. Visitors at the Rio Grande location said they saw adobe buildings that had many rooms and two or more floors, built much like pueblos of other Southwestern tribes. These homes were very permanent, but the Jumano hunters built grass huts that could be erected quickly when they were away from their home. Since the hunters came to the villages along the Rio Grande and visited the gardener Jumanos, it isn't known if they were related or not.

W. W. Newcomb in his book, *Indians of Texas*, agrees that there were several different bands of Jumano Indians. He states that the gardener branch of the Jumanos lived in villages stretching from El Paso all the way down the Rio Grande valley as far as the Big Bend region of Texas. In Chihuahua, Mexico the mouth of the Rio Concho flows into the Rio Grande at the present-day town of Oginaga. The town called Presidio is across the river on the Texas side. This point where the two rivers converge was called La Junta. A very large flood plain reaches from this point up the Rio Grande to community of Ruidoso. The floodplain was also evident below La Junta downstream 30 miles to Redford. Two terraces rose 20 to 60 feet above the floodplain. The wise Jumanos who settled there, lived on the terraces so they would be safe from floods and still farm the rich soil in the floodplain below their homes. They could find fish to catch and gather wild edible plants that grew in this area. The dessert like conditions along the Rio Grande and its 10.8 inches of yearly rain made it important to search for a variety of foods. The first Spaniards to visit their villages said their farms were plentiful, but they saw no means of irrigation ditches. The Indians depended on run-off water and rainfall. They raised corn, beans, squash, sunflowers and sometimes cultivated cotton and tobacco.

Some tribes of Indians occupied this area along the Rio Grande for a long time. Archeologists think it was first settled in 1200 A.D., but they think those early settlers could have been a different Indian tribe from the Jumano. Some scholars who studied this area think that 3,000 to 4,000 Jumano, along with other tribes, could have lived on the banks of the Rio Grande at the LaJunta location at one time. But Howard G. Applegate wrote "The Demography of LaJunta de Los Rios del Norte y

Conchos," in *The Journal of Big Bend Studies*. He stated that a particular area like this could have sustained as many as 10,000 inhabitants.

But this estimate is difficult to comprehend when one thinks of the arid conditions that existed just a short distance from the floodplains. When Cabeza de Vaca visited LaJunta, he said the Jumano hadn't planted corn for two years because of the drought. He also noticed a different way they used to cook food. He said they dropped a hot stone into a gourd where their uncooked food was deposited. The stones did the cooking. They were a nomadic tribe to some extent and by using the gourds, they didn't have to carry heavy pottery from one place to another.

If there were 10,000 Indians scattered along the Rio Conchos and Rio Grande, the population of this group was similar to the pueblo population in New Mexico. When these Indians, who lived several hundred miles northwest of La Junta, got tired of Spanish rule and revolted August 10, 1680, they numbered about 15,000.

Some evidence in Mexico suggests that the people at La Junta weren't the earliest people in that region. Many other tribes moved about including the Casa Grande Indians. Their villages and canal systems suggest that they dated back to prehistoric times. The Casas Grandes lived some 200 miles west of La Junta, in the interior of Mexico. They also built multi-storied buildings like some of the Jumanos did. This earlier tribe had a highly developed system of irrigation, which was verified by the archeological remains. What caused their demise is unknown. Maybe changing weather patterns much like that in pueblos farther west could have made the difference.

The Jumanos had one trade route that reached from northern Mexico to San Antonio to New Braunsfel and San Marcos, which were towns in Central Texas. Some reports indicate that the Plains Jumanos traded eastward from Central Texas. They had buffalo meat and skins to trade. The New Mexico Jumanos had obsidian, a mineral for making tools;

some salt, and sometimes turquoise. They also took pueblo pottery from New Mexico to trade eastward.

What is so astounding is that these traders had no horses at this time, but they made journeys of 500 miles or more. They walked to visit the other tribes in Texas. The Jumanos carried their wares in baskets or on their back. Jumanos also used dogs to transport their possessions. The dogs were rigged with a travois much like horses did in later years. One pole on each side of their body was connected to a strap that came around the chest of the dog. The two poles dragged behind the dog and could carry necessary bedding or food. The traders crisscrossed Texas from east to west, but their journeys were slow as they walked from place to place. Most of their trading occurred before the Comancheros came to Texas, so they didn't have too much competition. Comancheros were Mexicans living in the area who carried trade goods to the Indian tribes.

The Jumanos also knew how to mine salt, so they used it to trade for goods they needed. Little is written about the Jumanos attacking another tribe, so life was good for them at this time. But as early as 1525 the Apaches came to the plains of Texas. Such a warring tribe had a different method of existence. Little if any farming was done by the Apache. They fought for their position on the plains, so the Apaches quickly slowed down the trading done by the Jumanos. When these warriors appeared on the Texas plains, the peace-loving Jumanos had to go on the defense. The Apaches tried to conquer the Jumanos and push them out of their homes that they had built in Tejas country.

Although many Indian tribes seemed to let the females do all the manual labor, the pueblo Jumanos were different in that they divided the labor. Men worked in the fields while the women kept house, ground the corn and made beautiful baskets and pottery. The Jumano history reminds one of the pueblo tribes of the southwestern states because the Jumanos lived in stone or adobe houses, which had many rooms. Jumanos seemed to succeed along the Rio Grande until climate change, and maybe more Indian tribes entered their area.

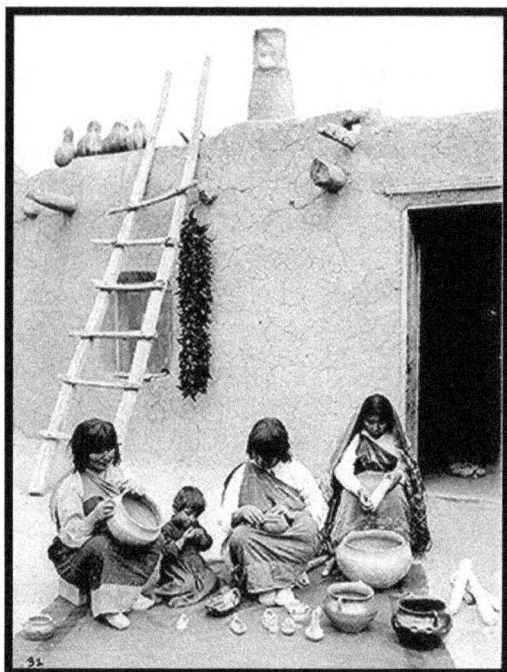

Indians in the Santa Clara Pueblo in New Mexico making pottery. Jumanos may have traveled to this pueblo to trade for pottery. Courtesy of the U. S. National Archives

The Jumano women wore long dresses, deerskin ponchos, but the men wore very little clothing. Only in cold weather did they use buffalo skins to keep them warm. The females wore their hair long, but the men either cut a portion of their hair or they wore it short in a bowl shape. Some of the Indians had jewelry made of copper, turquoise and coral. While the Jumanos were moving about Texas, men in armor and on horseback were moving about also. The Spanish explorers told their superiors

Ruins of Pueblo Missions in New Mexico. Sharon Gentry, along with Lewis and Christ Barton visited the ruins in 1967. Author's collection.

about the land they visited in New Mexico and Texas, so the Spanish eventually established a religious Franciscan monastery in Albuquerque. One day in 1623, twelve Jumano Indians showed up at the monastery and requested that they be baptized. Fray Juan De Salas who worked there was a bit overwhelmed because he had never seen this tribe of Indians. His visitors also wanted missionaries to be sent to their country so they could continue their Christian education. Residents at the monastery could hardly believe their request because no missionaries had ever been sent to the part of Texas that the Jumanos described as their home. The priest wondered how these Indians could know about Jesus and missionaries.

The following story the Jumanos told the priests has been thoroughly criticized, analyzed, and studied, but the conclusion most people reach is that it is true.

The Jumanos visitors told the priest that they had learned about Jesus Christ from a pale woman called, "Lady In Blue," who had visited them. Fray De Salas had no missionaries to spare, so he denied their request for assistance. The Jumanos sent a delegation to Albuquerque for the next six years, but each time they made the long trip, they were denied. The priest had no way of knowing what had happened back in 1620. According to the story, at that time, an 18-year-old nun from Spain named Mary said that she had mystic raptures during her meditations.

Mary shared her adventure with her spiritual supervisor and her other sisters at the convent. She said she made trips across the ocean as often as four times a month. Mary explained that she talked to the Indians in their own tongue, and they understood her. The Jumanos asked for a missionary on their trips because Mary had told them to request one. The Indians said she descended from the heavens and preached to them. She also told them how to build crosses, make rosaries, and erect a house of worship.

Sister Mary was from the same order as the priests at Albuquerque were, the Franciscan. Mary was of the Franciscan Order of Agreda in Spain. Mary continued to describe detailed versions of her travels to the New World, so in 1622 the Franciscan Minister General asked her to tell him about her spiritual raptures. To his surprise, she was very humble and sincere. He felt she was telling the truth, so over a period of time he decided to verify her experiences. It wasn't until 1626 that a letter was written from Mary's convent to the Archbishop of Mexico to see if Mary really visited the Jumanos in the New Land across the sea.

The Archbishop of Mexico sent an inquiry to Father Benavides, the Superior of the Franciscan Mission of New Mexico. A personal emissary, Father Perea, carried the letter from Mexico City to Albuquerque. During the time that the emissary was visiting, the delegation of Jumanos came to New Mexico on their annual trek. When the group asked for baptism this time, the Father was much more interested in their requests. When they talked of their Lady In Blue, they were asked if she looked anything like a portrait they had at the monastery of a nun of Franciscan Order. The Indians said their clothes were alike but their Lady in Blue was much younger than the picture.

Father Perea and two other priests decided to go back with the Jumanos to visit their home, which was probably near present-day San Angelo where the three rivers met. While this group was making the trek across the plains in 1629, the Lady in Blue was guiding the other Jumano bands to congregate together in one place. When the group from New Mexico returned home, they saw several thousand Indians coming to greet them. The mass of Indians knelt down and kissed the crosses. The priests couldn't believe what they saw.

Many more Indians came to the masses that were held in the ensuing days. The meeting at the three rivers was the first mass held in that area of Texas. The priests thought they may have witnessed a congregation of 60,000 Indians in all. The priests were overwhelmed, but they decided to return to New Mexico and make future plans to send missionaries to the Jumano Indians. Before the priests could leave, the Indians brought their sick to be healed and their request was granted.

Because the Jumanos had begged for the priests to come live with them for a long time, their wish finally became a reality. In 1632 a mission of Franciscans under Spanish rule was founded in this area. The mission was led by friars Juan de Salas and Juan de Ortega. According to Henry Bolton, a noted Texas historian, the mission near San Angelo was established in 1632, and that was the first mission in Texas. Bishop Michael Pfeiffer and the Catholic community of San Angelo have accepted this revelation and tried to honor the deeds of those responsible for it happening. Ortega stayed for six months, but the mission failed. This area was also visited by Castillo-Martin Expedition in 1650 and later in 1654, the Diego de Guadalajara Expedition came through the area.

Eventually emissaries from New Mexico traveled to Spain to tell the King of Spain what they had witnessed in New

Mexico. Father Benavides' report about the Blue Lady was entitled "Memorial of 1630" and it became a most important document about the New World. Since Mary of Agreda had talked to the Minister General, he could tell Father Benavides who to visit. They arrived in 1631, and Mary told Father Benavidez everything about her experiences in the New World. She could explain the looks of the one-eyed Captain Tuerto, the leader of the Jumanos. His name translates as "blind," and he was blind in one eye. The Blue Lady also explained the route of their travel and the detailed appearance of the tattooed Indians as well as how their countryside looked.

Mary of Agreda was born in 1602 and never left Spain. When she told her superior about her trances, she could have easily been condemned for witchcraft and been burned at the stake. She took a big chance when she told her story about visiting the New World.

But Benavides knew that Sister Mary truly had spiritual powers. He was a believer. Mary stopped her raptures to the southwestern part of the New World in 1631. But she continued her visions and powerful insights for many more years. Mary carried on a correspondence with the Hapsburg king, King Phillip IV from 1843 until she died in 1665. Mary advised him both politically and spiritually for twenty-two years. There is documented evidence of this correspondence that included over 600 letters. Mary was buried in a glass coffin, and her body refused to decay for the over 300 years she has been entombed. Many skeptical historians have studied this event and came away saying there is too much evidence to say it didn't happen.

Toward the later part of the 1600s, the Jumanos fell on hard times. Several different theories have come into play as to how the Jumano tribe shrank in size. One theory is that the influence of the Spanish explorers had something to do with their demise. Archeologist Eric Shroeder, who was studying at the University of Texas, gave a speech September 26, 2013 in San Angelo, Texas about the Jumano tribe. He suggested that the influence of the Spaniards on the Jumano was not good.

Shroeder said that the Spaniards gave the Indians cheap cotton blankets in exchange for buffalo hides of greater value. He explained that the hides were made into shoes by workmen in the small villages of Tejas country.

Shroeder also suggested that the Spaniards didn't see the Jumano tribe as all being on the same social level. The Spanish traders catered to the higher social level of the tribe. Chiefs had nicer pottery and jewelry than the working class did. They also had horses to ride and guns, which were possessions the lesser tribe members didn't have. Shroeder suggests that although Jumano men and women previously shared the work, there may have now been a working class of Jumanos. Women, children, and lower class men prepared the buffalo hides and made the pemmican food from dried meat.

Eric Shroeder studied the location of middens in the areas where Jumanos likely camped. Most middens, refuse dumps, are in areas near water sources where the whole tribe would camp. However, he found middens in secluded places away from the water sources. And these middens suggested a small group camped there. His explanation for these locations was that Spanish leaders may have provided feasts for the leaders of the tribe, and in that way, they alienated the working class from the chiefs. Could this power play have divided the Jumanos and caused the cohesiveness of the tribe to decrease?

If the Spanish influence wasn't the villain, then other warring tribes may have been. Some historians think that the Jumano tribes were attacked by stronger warriors such as the Apache, and this loss caused their number to dwindle. Having small numbers in their tribe left them vulnerable to Spanish raids. The very same people who had visited with the Jumano in the early years of exploration now came to Texas to collect slaves to work in their silver mines and agricultural fields. The silver mines were located at Parral, Chihuahua.

It was a terrible situation where some of the captured Jumanos were taken two hundred miles into the interior of Mexico to work as slaves. Working in the mines was a brutal environment, and many Indians died over the years until the surviving ones finally began to fight back. In 1689 a revolt took place in northern Mexico, and the workers were finally free. The missions at places like La Junta closed down. A few years later the Mexicans tried to revive their missionary work, but it wasn't successful.

Juan Sabeata was a fascinating Jumano warrior who led the tribe in its later years. In 1683, he asked the governor who lived in El Paso to send priests to the La Juanta area along the Rio Grande. He explained that his tribe wanted to become Christians. He had another request: he wanted the Spanish to help his people defend themselves from the aggressive Apache. So in 1683-84, Juan Dominguez de Mendoza led an expedition from Mexico that had several goals. First, they wanted to search the southwestern portion of Texas for good water sources. They had 20 New Mexican troops from El Paso with them, and of course they had hired a guide named Juan Sabeata. Another goal was to set up churches, so Friar Nicolas Lopez accompanied the expedition according to *The Native Americans of the Texas Edwards Plateau* by Maria F. Wade. Although the Mexican government had named Sabeata as a governor of the area, they used him also to lead them through the area they wanted to explore. When the expedition came to La Juanta, the Indians showed them a thatched roof church they had built. Mendoza left four priests and several soldiers at La Juanta before he directed the rest of his group to ride north.

He wanted to find the place where the Concho Rivers flowed into one stream. The Mexicans also had Indians of several different tribes riding with them. One of the objectives of the trip was to meet with representatives of thirty tribes. These Indians hoped to make treaties with Spain so that the aggressive Apaches could be halted. The Expedition came to where two rivers met, and called it El Angel de Guarda. This location was believed to have been where the North and South Concho Rivers meet, which is the location of modern day San Angelo, Texas.

The expedition stayed at this camp for seven days, February 12 through February 18, 1684. They explored the area and found so many pearls in the Concho River that they named it the River of Pearls. Buffalo were very common in this area since it was their usual location to range along the rivers during the winter months. Mendoza's men had a chance to stock up on buffalo meat, so they shot eighty buffalo while camped along the Concho River. The troops also found turkeys, catfish, nuts, and camotes. This latter food is probably an edible tuber.

Mendoza wasn't completely happy with his guide, Sabeata, because he felt that the Jumano Chief, Sabeata, wanted the Mendoza-Lopez Expedition to help him fight his enemy the Apaches. By this time, the number of Jumanos had decreased sharply, and they couldn't protect themselves from the aggressive Apache. Sabeata had worked hard to supply the expedition with food and other things they needed along the way, but he couldn't convince Mendoza that the Apache were about to attack the Expedition. When Mendoza had started this trip, Governor Cruzates had given specific orders to find this place where the rivers came together. Since Mendoza had reached his goal when he found the Concho Rivers, he didn't need the Jumano Chief anymore. Sabeata was released of his scouting and guide duties.

But Sabeata stayed busy during 1684 because he was able to encourage the Franciscans from New Mexico to establish missions called LaNavidad en las Cruces and Apostol Santiago. These missions were for the Jumanos at LaJunta on the Rio Grande. The Jumano Chief also wanted to help refugees who were fleeing from the Apaches. Although Sabeata lived at LaJunta, for ten years he led the Jumanos on "trade fairs" with other Indians who lived in central and eastern Texas. When he wasn't making a hot trade, Sabeata was busy finding recruits for his cause. One group of men who he enlisted to help him were the Ciboleros. They were really Mexican buffalo hunters who hunted periodically for their family and community. How Sabeata reined them into joining his war party is unknown.

Since the Jumano couldn't whip the Apaches, they finally strove to integrate with them. By 1729, the alliance was successful enough that the Spanish referred to the two tribes as one, the Jumano-Apache.

Since the Jumanos and the Lady in Blue is associated with the San Angelo area of Texas, various Catholic leaders have worked to honor the Jumano tribe. Bishop Michel Pfeiffer of San Angelo has been helpful in bringing recognition to them. When there seems to be no more interest in the project, another miracle appears in history to spur on renewed activity.

The year 2005 had an unusual event happen that was explained by tribal historian Enrique Madrid. That year a gigantic blue bonnet plant, over five feet in height, was seen in the Big Bend area of Texas. Finding this huge bluebonnet reminded Enrique of the legend of the bluebonnet. When the Lady in Blue told the Jumano Indians that her visits to them would cease, she also told them that they were to seek baptism from the missionary fathers. The Indians said she had been standing on a hillside when she spoke to them and suddenly they noticed that the area was covered with bluebonnet flowers. Enrique Madrid, author of *Maria of Agreda: Mystical Lady in Blue,* said that when she saw the large bluebonnet, she knew that the Lady in Blue had come back to help the Jumano tribe. Her people have survived she believes because of their Christian faith and willingness to unite with other tribes and go underground for their own protection when necessary. Now many years later, the Jumanos are working to re-establish their tribal identity with the U.S. Bureau of Indian Affairs. Under the name Jumano-Apache they have registered 400 to 500 members. Tribal chieftain Gabriel Carrasco says there are probably 1,000 to 2,000 more members, but when they are scattered throughout Texas and other states, it is hard to get the word out. He says, "...we are encouraged because we believe the Lady in Blue is telling us now that 'it is time for the Jumanos to come forward'."

Location in San Angelo, Texas where Concho Rivers come together. Marker commemorates the work of Juan de Ortega and of the Blue Lady. Author's Collection.

JUMANO

Although Jumanos often displayed body drawings, this man is covered by a buffalo robe.

Ch. 5 Kiowa Indians

The early Kiowa people lived in the cold, northwestern areas of America. With only dogs to transport their equipment, their circle of existence at this time was a very small area. We know this much about the tribe because they kept pictographic calendars of events that happened during their history. Their movements across America were also chronicled in monthly and yearly calendars.

As time passed, they moved southeastward and made friends with the Crow tribe. There was some intermarriage with this friendly tribe. Kiowa warriors walked everywhere they went until they met up with the Crow tribe who introduced the Kiowa to the fabulous horse. Riding lessons must have been a fun thing to watch because the pride of the warrior was on display as he tried to mount a fidgety horse without getting dumped off. But it didn't take very long before the Crow warriors taught the Kiowa how to ride these ponies and fly through the hills and valleys.

Soon the Kiowa tribe became more independent and on the move. As they traveled farther south, they met up with buffalo. Once they learned to kill them, they had both food and clothing from the huge, shaggy animal. Eventually they visited with the Spaniards and acquired slaves and guns. This once insignificant tribe now became the most feared of all who roamed the plains. They committed warfare on anyone who stood in their way.

If a person could get close enough to a Kiowa without losing their life, they noticed these Indians had distinct appearances and ways of living. Their braves were tall and walked with a graceful gait as they showed off their long hair. Both men and women wore skin garments, moccasins, leggings, and fur robes if it was cold. They collected Mexican silver coins and fashioned jewelry from them. Men always wore their hair braided, but women either braided their hair or wore it loose. Lone Wolf's portrait details the fine Roman outline of his head.

The Kiowa tribe had a definite system of ranking people within their tribe. The top ranked Indians were the aristocrats. They included great warriors, sub-chiefs, ten priests who took care of the medicine bundles, and wealthy tribesmen associated with war or religion. The second rank included lesser medicine men, those who took care of the ill and practiced magic, small sub-chiefs, and people of limited property. The third rank included the poor people of the tribe, which included about half of the Kiowa people. The last rank was the misfits or crazy people. It was possible in their society to move up or down the ranks. When you get right down to the facts, the Kiowa rankings in social order may not be very different from what we Americans observe in our culture today.

The Kiowa ate mostly meat but supplemented that with fruits, berries, roots, and nuts. Their tall teepees were covered with buffalo hides. Not only were their homes easy to transport but also their cooking utensils, which included hide bags and containers. Horns of animals were carved into spoons but no pottery was used. When they wanted to boil water to cook their meal, they heated stones in the fire until they were red-hot. Then the stones were dropped into skin bags filled with water. Many stones were heated this way until the food was cooked to their satisfaction.

Through the years, the Kiowa Indian tribe was blessed with several leaders who worked for peace, and not so blessed by those who advocated war. Some people may not know that within one tribe there could be several chiefs at the same time, but that was true of the Kiowa. In tribal government, the Kiowa had a head or civil chief who was very important. He was the camp leader chosen by all the Topadoks, the Kiowa people. The war chiefs were chosen by the council. Kiowa Chief Dohason was a peace loving man who lived from the 1790s to 1866. He was the last great chief who bound the tribe together in unity. A little later, the tribe leaders included Lone Wolf who was born about 1820 and died in 1879, and Kicking Bird who lived from 1835 to 1875. There was a split in allegiance between these two younger chiefs because Kicking Bird strove for peace while Lone Wolf fought the invading white man. These two men overlapped their leadership sometimes, so both were

serving the tribe at the same time. Kicking Bird, of Crow-Kiowa descent, lived as a young boy in western Oklahoma, in the Texas Panhandle, and in southwestern Kansas. Quickly he became a well-known warrior even in his youth. Leadership traits surfaced in him also at a young age. By 1865, Kicking Bird was only 30 years old, but he led the peace faction of the Kiowa braves. He signed the Little Arkansas Treaty that year. A large number of tribes signed this treaty including Kiowas, Comanche, Plains Apache, Southern Cheyenne, and Southern Arapaho. The reason the government pushed this treaty to be signed was because white settlers wanted peace along the Santa Fe Trail. But the Indian tribes wanted unlimited hunting ground. Indians had reservations south of the Arkansas River. When treaties were signed, there was often times exchange of prisoners. This time the Box family, which included a woman and four children, from Texas was released at a location in Kansas where the treaty was signed. But none of the agreements of this treaty were put in practice by the U.S.

Kicking Bird from the Kiowa and other Indians found themselves at the treaty table one year later to redo the old agreement. Now the U. S. Government pushed the Medicine Lodge Treaty of 1867, which was also negotiated in Kansas. This time the government was armed with five hundred U. S. soldiers under command of Major Joel H. Elliot and a newly formed Indian Peace Commission that Congress had created.

Under this treaty, the Kiowa, Comanche, and Plains Apache released 60,000 square miles of territory for a reservation only 3 million acres in size. The tribes were also given $30,000 worth of houses, barns, and schools that they hadn't requested. Ten Kiowa chiefs signed this treaty including Satank, Satanta, and Kicking Bird.

By this time, Kicking Bird was known as a chief who stood for peace, so he strove not to fight anymore than he had to. While Kicking Bird was trying to make peace at the meeting in Kansas, George Armstrong Custer was at nearby Fort Leavenworth. The flashy Custer was fighting as usual, but this time he was fighting his own court martial. After the court proceedings were over and he won, Custer came out as arrogant as ever. A short time later, some of the Kiowa tribe took part in the Battle of the Washita in 1868, and Maj. Gen. George A. Custer swore that Kicking Bird was part of the fighting warriors, but Kicking Bird swore that he wasn't. When the young chief didn't fight, some of the Kiowa warriors said that Kicking Bird was a coward. To set matters straight, Kicking Bird decided to show his critics that he was still a leader. Kicking Bird prepared for a journey and led a raid into Texas in 1870, but he never fought again after they returned.

On February 18, 1872, Kicking Bird met a Quaker teacher named Thomas C. Battey. The chief was so impressed by the teacher that he urged him to come to his camp and teach his daughter, Topen. Kicking Bird wanted Battey to live in the Kiowa camp, but at first Battey was afraid of the Indians and their customs. After being reassured by the tribal leaders, Battey decided to give it a try. Kicking Bird's brother, Ze'bile invited Battery to share his lodge. Classes started January 23, 1873. Battey said he had a hard time at first because of the language barrier, and the fact that he had to contend with constant onlookers. Some Indians were just curious about the white man's school while others interfered with the classroom by their presence. Teacher Battey had to discuss reading and writing with a curious crowd of Indian onlookers.

Even though some English was taught in the Kiowa camp, a few teepees had militant Indians holding council and planning another raid while school was taking place nearby. Some of the Kiowa warriors who were determined to fight the white man led an uprising in 1874-75. Kicking Bird refused to take part in the fighting and protected his remaining people who were peaceful at this time. The army officers were aware of his authority over the tribe, so when some of the fighting Kiowa men were captured by the army, the officers went to the Kiowa camp and asked Kicking Bird for help. The U.S. Army had decided to send some of the captives that caused the most trouble to Florida. Rather than do the dirty work themselves, the officers asked Kicking Bird to select 70 Kiowa captives to be sent on this journey. This demand put Kicking Bird in an awkward position, because he wanted to be fair to his own tribe, but at the same time, he tried to help the white men. He picked White Horse, Maman-ti, Lone Wolf, and a number of less known Kiowas, Comanches, Cheyennes, Arapahos, and Mexicans.

When the young chief helped the army by picking out warriors to go into captivity, some of his fellow tribesmen felt he was a traitor. Then to make matters worse, the officials at Fort Sill presented Kicking Bird with a fine grey horse, and this present caused the rumors to spread even more. His fellow Kiowa warriors thought he was a traitor. Kicking Bird met his death in a strange way because he was probably poisoned. Most likely his sudden death after drinking a cup of coffee on May 3, 1875 was brought about by some of his militant Kiowa enemies. He was buried in the Fort Sill Cemetery.

Another Kiowa Chief who took a different approach to leadership was Chief Lone Wolf. He lived at a time when his tribe roamed over a large area of the Southwestern United States. He led his warriors from the mountains of Colorado to the Texas Plains and into Mexico. Although he was ready to challenge any string of blue-coated soldiers he encountered while traveling through Texas, he was still involved in peace negotiations as much as any chief. Lone Wolf made two trips to Washington D.C. in his lifetime trying to make a peace treaty with the Great White Father.

While Lone Wolf was their leader, the Kiowas often pitched their tents near the buildings at Fort Bent, a location coinciding with modern day La Junta, Colorado. Other tribes such as the Cheyenne, the Apache, and Comanche lived in this area also. William Bent owned the trading post there and had a

Cheyenne wife. He wanted all the Indians of the area to live in peace, so a lasting treaty was made in 1840 that was never broken. But many years later, one event concerning Indian teepees almost bent the peace treaty to its breaking point though.

In the summer of 1856, the Kiowas left their teepees in care of William Bent, who ran Bent's Fort, while they went on a buffalo hunt. When they returned, they were very upset because Bent had given their tents to the Cheyennes. Soon a battle erupted. Lone Wolf's horse was shot in the fight and his braves had to retreat. But the Kiowas later made peace with the Cheyennes, who probably were called the "house robbers."

The Kiowa tribe was religious in that they believed in supernatural beings. In early summer, the tribe always celebrated the Sun Dance, a celebration that lasted ten days. Six of these days were in preparation as they set up a special lodge, the center post, and had a mock battle before the dedication portion of the ceremony. Four days were taken to dance about the pole and seek visions. Sometimes self-inflicted torture was included as they cut themselves or broke fingers. Once the ceremony was over, they dismantled camp and moved. If their vision included a raid, the warriors would leave immediately to complete the vision. Sun Boy was a mythic figure who gave them medicine in ten portions. It was kept in Grandmother Bundles by the priests in their teepees. The Sun Dance worship was believed to create the buffalo so they would have food. The ceremony also rededicated the tribe's beliefs and traditions. Another type of worship involved eating the buds of cactus. These buds contained peyote, which has proven to bring about hallucinations.

By the 1850s more wagon trains were crossing over land where the Kiowas and their friends roamed. As settlers came under Indian attack, the government had to do something. They knew the area needed protection. The First Dragoons were sent to accompany wagon trains through Santa Fe, and later the Second Dragoons and the Mounted Rifles tried to hold back the Kiowa and their friends, but they did little good in stopping them.

Once the Kiowa warrior was mounted, a few changes took place in the tools that he used. When they were hunting on horseback, they used a shortened bow that was easier to handle than the long one. They also tied everything they owned either on the saddle or on a bigger travois that they pulled behind a horse. All containers were made of hides, so they could travel without breaking anything. When the decision to move was announced in camp, a band of Kiowa could move in 30 minutes. The real marvel of this fact is that the women in camp tore down the teepees and packed everything quickly enough to suit the men folks.

By 1863, Lone Wolf was a member of the Tsetanma, an elite society of warriors, which gave him much privilege. His fighting ability and leadership earned him the right to represent his tribe when he made a trip to Washington, D.C. with Indian agent S.G. Colley. Although this attempt to obtain peace for the Kiowa and other tribes failed, in 1865 he was one of several chiefs who signed the Little Arkansas Treaty with federal commissioners October 18, 1865.

But signing such a treaty didn't keep his tribe from riding to Texas to look for horses. A scarce six months after the signing, the Kiowa were in the saddle riding fast to capture 150 ponies from Texas owners. They traveled light on such trips and seldom stopped for a meal. They carried a ready-made meal in a pouch that probably resembled a tobacco pouch in size. It contained pemmican, a mixture of dried meat and fruit that was mixed with tallow.

There's no doubt that the Kiowa women prepared this food for the warriors to use. Almost all the work around the camp was done by the women. They collected berries and other edible food, skinned the buffalo brought to camp, sewed their garments, and cooked the meals. The warrior's job was to protect the camp, but they spent most of the time sitting around smoking. One squaw admitted that the men were pretty good babysitters.

The men also had to handle any treaties or meetings that involved the tribe. Although Kicking Bird and other Kiowa Chiefs signed the treaty at Medicine Lodge, Kansas in 1857, Lone Wolf didn't. He was wise enough about these treaties that he suspected if he signed this one, he couldn't raid anymore ranches or steal horses, so he refused to make his mark on the treaty. He reasoned that having horses kept his tribe independent, so he could raid and war against the U.S. Cavalry a few more years.

Chief Satanta of the Kiowas was another important chief of their tribe. He was an impressive figure with broad shoulders to match his tall physique. He could lead others with his eloquent voice. He spoke four Indian languages as well as Spanish and English. In *The American Story: Defiant Chiefs* by Time Life, a government doctor told of his visit with Satanta at his village on the Arkansas River. The doctor was inoculating the Indians against smallpox because in previous outbreaks of the disease many Indians had died of it. The doctor described Satanta as "a fine-looking Indian, very energetic and sharp as a briar." The chief made his guests feel very welcome because he fixed a carpet for them to sit on and blew his brass horn when it was time for meals.

But life for this amiable Indian began to change very fast when the white settlers came westward and invaded the land that the Indians held so dear. Satanta began to fight the oncoming settlers, and he was quoted as saying, "I love the land and the buffalo and will not part with it." But the invasion of settlers decreased the number of game as well as the prairie grasses for the animals to eat. When Satanta saw this happening, he said, "I feel as though my heart will burst with sorrow."

Then Lone Wolf and Chief Satanta met with a brash young cavalry leader named Lt. Col., George Custer in 1868. After the peace talks, Custer invited the two leaders to Fort

Cobb in Oklahoma. This fort was on an Indian Reservation. Satanta and Lone Wolf were enticed to come to the fort under the promise of a flag of truce. But the moment they arrived, Gen. Phillip Sheridan ordered the two men be held hostage. Custer talked a different talk when he had them under custody and told the two chiefs that he would hang them if they didn't agree to return to the reservation. The military powers that be weren't very quick about releasing the two chiefs either. They languished in jail for about a year. During this time, Chief Kicking Bird tried to get them released. When they were finally allowed to go home, most of the tribe had returned to the reservation.

By 1871 the Kiowas were on their horses again and headed to Mexico. Chiefs Satanta, Satank, and Big Tree led about 100 Indians. On that expedition, the warriors attacked a wagon train at Salt Creek, which was 20 miles west of Fort Richardson, near the Oklahoma-Texas border. They killed the wagon master and seven teamsters before they took what they wanted from the wagons and headed back to the reservation.

In the newspaper, this atrocity was called the "Warren Wagon Train Raid," and Gen. William Sherman, along with some soldiers, immediately tracked down the culprits. Chiefs Satanta, Satank, and Big Tree were captured and in a few days they were put in a wagon to take them to Texas for trial. As they started on their journey, they were all three sitting with chains about their bodies. Satank began to sing his death chant. He knew every mile he travel took him farther from the bones of his beloved son whom he had lost.

Satank kept the bones of his son in a special teepee near his family teepee on the Reservation. As the wagon rumbled along, the aged chief pulled a concealed knife, leaped at the guard, and wrestled a carbine from him. Soldiers who saw the commotion instantly shot Chief Satank. But he lunged again toward the rifle and was shot again. He died a short time later at a creek that was named Sitting Bear Creek. This unusual name was used because it was another name for Chief Satank.

When the other two chiefs got to their trial, the court ruling at Fort Richardson condemned them to death. This trial is believed to be the first time an Indian was tried in a white man's court.

When a large number of Indians congregated to fight for their imprisoned leaders, the Texas Governor Edmund Davis decided that he had better diffuse the situation. Edmund Davis had fought on the Union side of the Civil War, but when the war was over, he decided to head to Texas to live. He ran successfully for governor of Texas in 1869. Now as governor, Edmund realized that holding these two chiefs in custody was asking for trouble, so the sentence given to Satanta and Big Tree was changed to life imprisonment, and two years later, he paroled the two chiefs. They were free to return to the reservation and live in peace. But neither of these men could stay put in their teepees very long. Big Tree's release was in 1873, and at that time, he promised to quit fighting the white man. But a year later he took two hundred warriors and attacked Gen. Miles and his supply train. This battle continued for three days, and several troopers were killed.

The Kiowa chiefs each spent their last days in a different way. Chief Satanta continued to raid until he was caught and sentenced to a prison term in Huntsville Prison in Texas. Satanta couldn't adjust to prison life, so he committed suicide in 1878 by jumping from a second-story balcony into the prison courtyard. He died a few hours later. Satanta explained his feelings one time when he was talking about his people. He said, "When we settle down, we grow pale and die." But Chief Big Tree looked at the changing world in a different way. He counseled his people to accept peace as the Indian wars came to a close. Big Tree converted to the Baptist faith and lived well into his eighties before passing away.

Lone Wolf could only stay so long on the reservation until the call of freedom took hold. In 1872 the Kiowa warriors visited the southwestern part of Texas, and Lone Wolf had his son, Sitting-in-the-Saddle with him. They attacked a wagon train at Howard's Well south of present-day Ozona, Texas. This stage station served the San Antonio-El Paso Road. In the attack, several teamsters driving their wagons were killed. The Ninth United States Cavalry from Fort Concho were in the area and heard about the Kiowa attack. The Cavalry located the Indians and opened fire. Lone Wolf's favorite son, Sitting-on-Saddle, was wounded in the battle with the soldiers, but he was rescued by a warrior named Mamadayte. Even though Lone Wolf gave the cavalry a run for their money, he was respected by the soldiers and their leaders. When it came time for the Indian agent named Henry Alford to go to Washington, he convinced Lone Wolf to accompany him. Two of Lone Wolf's friends, Chief Satanta and Chief Big Tree, were jailed.

On this trip in 1872, Lone Wolf was able to get his friends released. All ideas about staying on the reservation seemed to fly out the window in 1873, because Lone Wolf was at it again. On this trip he led his warriors into Mexico to raid down there. On his way home as he was passing through Texas, he fought the Fourth United States Cavalry at Kickapoo Springs in Edwards County. In that skirmish on December 10, 1873, his son, Sitting-in-the-Saddle, was killed.

Lone Wolf had to leave his son's body at the site of the battle, but this father couldn't get over his son's death. He mourned for Sitting-in-the-Saddle for a year and finally decided to return to the location of the battle. He found the remains of his dead loved one, loaded him probably on a travois, and traveled many miles to a spot that he remembered as a good burial site. Lone Wolf buried his son on a high hill in present-day Mitchell County near Loraine, Texas. The hill is now named Lone Wolf Mountain.

.

This loss of a son caused Lone Wolf to hate the white man even more, so he led many raids off the reservation. In 1874, the Kiowa braves took part in the second Adobe Walls battle June 27, 1874. About two weeks later, he attacked twenty-seven Texas Rangers in what was called the Lost Valley Fight. Two rangers were killed, and they lost most of their horses to none other than the Kiowa. During the battle, Kiowa warrior, Mamadyte, killed a ranger named David Bailey. He knew that David was the one who killed Lone Wolf's son a year before. After the battle, Mamadyte gave the dead soldier to Lone Wolf. The Chief cut off the ranger's head and said that his son was now avenged. For this brave deed in battle by Mamadyte, Lone Wolf adopted him and gave him the name Lone Wolf the Younger.

In 1874, Lone Wolf couldn't follow the peaceful existence of some Kiowas, so he led a band of warriors on a wagon train attack. But when the shooting began, the Kiowas had to flee in defeat because the train had more fire power than expected. Eventually the Kiowas decided to ride into Palo Duro Canyon for protection. They are another tribe whose story becomes entangled with a zealous soldier in this long canyon with many hiding places. A few days later, Col. Ranald S. Mackenzie led his troops down the slopes of the canyon walls and attacked every Indian in site. The Kiowa camp was destroyed so that when Lone Wolf and his men left the canyon, they took very little provisions with them. The weather was very cold on the plains and they had no food. Lone Wolf wandered around for awhile with his few men until he decided to turn himself in at Fort Sill on February 26, 1875. He was imprisoned and sent finally to Fort Marion in Florida. At this post, he contacted malaria and became very ill. Finally in the summer of 1879 he was released, and after he returned to the reservation, he died near Fort Sill.

A post-script to the story occurred in Mitchell County in 1902. At that time, local ranchers around Lone Wolf Mountain were surprised to see two wagon loads of Indians making their way to Lone Wolf Mountain, about four miles north of Loraine,

Texas. Area citizens also saw fires on top of the mountain at this time. Harvey Muns, who knew the story of their visit, recounted it by saying the Oklahoma Indians camped there for three days. After the Indians departed, area men visited the campgrounds and noticed that a large hole had been excavated on Lone Wolf Mountain. Since Lone Wolf also buried his nephew, Heart-of-a-young-wolf, at the same time that he buried his son, observers thought the Indians may have unearthed the bones of their ancestors and taken them back to Oklahoma with them.

In 1887 most of the Kiowas were living on the Indian Reservation in Oklahoma, but the white man didn't want the Indians to continue living on these valuable lands that white settlers wanted. By 1888 the U.S. Census listed 1,151 living Kiowas. But the white man wanted all the land, even the Reservation, so they set up a conference with the Indian leaders at Fort Sill on September 28, 1892. Lone Wolf the Younger attended this meeting with the federal commissioners from Washington. He had fought for his people to try to prevent the white man from killing all the buffalo. Lone Wolf had fought at Adobe Walls, but now he had to fight a legal battle of words.

According to *The American Story – Defiant Chiefs* by Time-Life Books, this commission from Washington was carrying out the wishes of Congress who had already passed an act in 1887 that said each Indian family would receive 160 acres and a single person would receive 80 acres of their rightful share of the Indian Reservation lands. What the commissioners didn't say in the meeting was that any remaining land on the Reservation could be sold to white settlers. Indians like Lone Wolf didn't want to divide their land. They remembered promises made to their people in years past that said they would never have to part with any Reservation land.

Lone Wolf the Younger finally got to speak before the agents there at Fort Sill. He said he felt that the government should not "push us ahead too fast on the road we are to take." Well known Comanche Quanah Parker was in the meeting also. He saw danger in changing things so quickly and he mentioned, "Do not go at this thing like you are riding a swift horse, but hold up a little."

Lone Wolf and other chiefs knew that when they received the Reservation land in the Medicine Lodge Treaty of 1867, the treaty stated that no changes would be made unless approved by three-quarters of the adult males. Such a vote would never have carried except that some people who weren't Indians placed a vote and other votes were forgeries. Lone Wolf and other leaders fought this case, called *Lone Wolf v. Hitchcock,* all the way to the Supreme Court. He sat in the gallery of the Supreme Court in 1902 when the case was heard. The court ruled against the Indians, and in five short years, all the tribal land became a part of the state of Oklahoma.

The Kiowa tribe didn't give up fighting the United States for rights and land they felt was theirs. In 1948 representatives from the Kiowa, Apache and Comanche tribes filed suit against the U.S. Government for compensation due them in unpaid cases. These charges rocked along through the courts for years, but the tribes eventually won compensation worth tens of millions of dollars from the Indian Claims Commission.

The Kiowa were an intelligent people who kept extensive records. They also developed a 37 month calendar. When they were forced to live the white man's way, these attributes helped them along the way.

It wasn't very long before the Kiowa people were challenged to live under new conditions. An unusual statistic is that more Kiowas were able to assimilate into the white man's culture than most other Indian groups. In fact, some were able to do that in one generation. Kiowas were very intelligent, and they wanted their children to be educated so they could follow the new ways and new language that was around them. Kiowa adults have been able to embrace the many occupations that the white man's world offered.

At the present time, the Kiowa Indians are alive and well. The Kiowa Tribe of Oklahoma now boasts of 12,000 members in 2013. Their headquarters is located at Carnegie, Oklahoma. This community is southwest of Oklahoma City. Nearby is the Caddo National Hall of Fame for Famous Indians. This is an outdoor exhibit with busts of the famous men. There is also the Southern Plains County Museum. The Washita River runs along this area, and Fort Cobb State Park is nearby. This area of Oklahoma has a lot of Indian history, which is made available for visitors to see. The town of Anadarko not only has the State Park nearby, but it also has the Indian Museum and Craft Center nearby.

The Kiowa tribe also has a casino at Devol, Oklahoma. The tribe encourages their members to continue speaking the Kiowa language, and they have workshops from time to time to help members with language challenges.

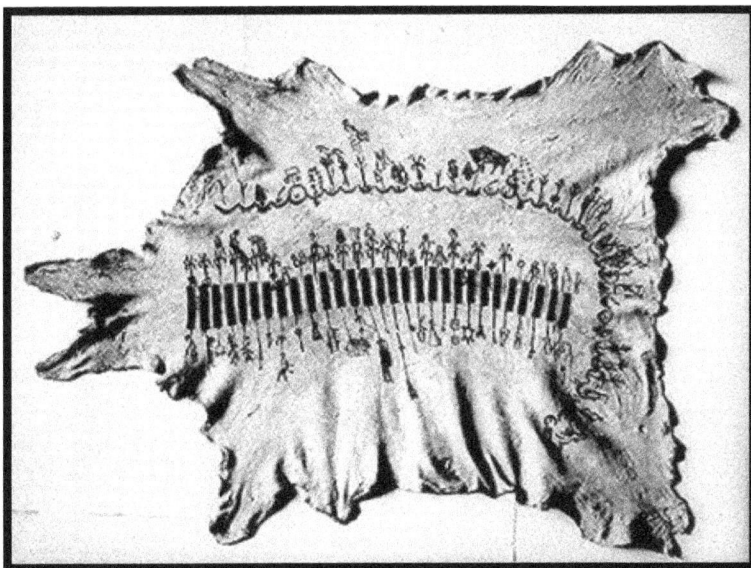

The 37- month Kiowa calendar. Courtesy of the U. S. National Archives

Recently a historic vote took place in the Kiowa Tribe in Oklahoma. They selected a female chairwoman for the first time. According to the *Native American Times,* Charging-after-the-Enemy, a thirty-seven year-old tribe member is now taking the reins of leadership in the Kiowa tribe. Her legal name is Amber Toppah, and this well-educated woman mentioned in her interview that she is hoping to work successfully with the council to improve communication, spirituality, and passion. She hopes harmony will prevail when it comes time to make important decisions. Amber is the great-great-granddaughter of Chief Satanta and the daughter of Carol Bearbow Toppah (Kiowa/Cheyenne) and the late Byron Toppah (Kiowa.)

Chief Lone Wolf, leader of the Kiowa tribe, who was a War Chief for the tribe even though he went to Washington D.C. attempting to make peace . Courtesy of the U.S. National Archives.

Kicking Bird was a peace seeking Kiowa Chief. Photo by William Soule in 1870. Courtesy of the U.S. National Archives

Satana, also called White Bear, was a Kiowa Chief. Courtesy of the U.S. National Archives.

Ch. 6 Lipan Indians

Although the name "Lipan" stands for a distinct Indian tribe, in recent history they became associated with Apaches, hence we know them as Lipan Apache at this time. The Lipan tribe belonged to the Southern Athabascan Indian tribe who loved to roam the southern plains on their fast horses. Since they were known for moving about quite often, their war bonnets might be hung temporarily in Texas, New Mexico, Colorado, or the northern part of Mexico. Although the Lipans spent their early years in the northwestern part of the U.S., they set up their teepees quite early in Texas. Spanish settlers around San Antonio mention the Lipans in their records in 1718 and it wasn't because of their good deeds. The Lipan Apache raided homes in San Antonio.

Another group of men in Tejas country had a different goal to reach that involved the Lipans. Undeterred by the Lipan raids, Catholic Fathers were bent on saving the Indian's soul, so they continued to lay plans for a mission near the area that the Indians migrated. Some years later the Spanish built a mission in Coahuila, Mexico in 1754 and on the San Saba River in 1757. As the word of God was preached in these buildings, the Lipan Apaches were among several tribes who visited the missionaries and listened to their sermons. Although the Lipan Apaches showed up at both of these missions, other Indian tribes weren't so pleased with the presence of the Spanish and their coddling the Lipans. These militant tribes burned down the missions and destroyed them completely.

The Comanches were present at that horrific event and very involved in torching the missions. They were the one tribe who hit the Texas Plains with intent to rule it with force. When the Comanche warriors routed the Great Plains and killed everyone who looked like a competitor for the grass and buffalo, the Lipan Apaches took notice. Teepees came down and the Lipan Apaches decided their next address would be somewhere farther south toward Mexico. When the Lipans headed south in 1750, they divided into several different bands.

An encampment of Lipan Indians possibly during Chief Flacco's time.

Most historians believe there were as many as 6,000 Lipan Apaches in Texas by 1700, but each band lived apart from the others except when they joined together in an all out war against their enemies . Then they wanted a lot of warriors.

Although the Lipans were putting distance between them and the Comanche, they couldn't stay out of battle for very long. This tribe of Lipans seemed to know where the fight was taking place and nearly always got themselves involved. About the same time that the tribe was accused of being the favorite tribe around the San Saba Mission, they were in battle with the Hasinais Confederation. According to W. W. Newcomb, Jr. in his book, *The Indians of Texas*, this was a very large group of eight tribes who fought together when necessary, and they lived between the Neches and Angelina Rivers in East Texas. They included tribes such as Hainai, Neches, Nacogdoches, Nacono, Namidish, Nasoni, and Anadarko.

The Lipan Apache were also known as one of the few tribes who helped the prevailing country that happened to own Texas at that time. Ownership of Tejas country in those early years changed from Spain, to Mexico and finally to the Republic of Texas. When the Spanish Expedition was formed in 1759 to fight the Wichita and the Comanche, the Lipans sided with the Spanish.

But not all the Spanish people liked all the Indian tribes, and vice versa. Even so, the Lipans found themselves so dependent on the Spanish that they lived near their missions. The Lipans felt that they needed the protection of the missionaries. After a while, this relationship between the Indians and the Spanish didn't work very well for the Lipans. The people at the missions seemed to try to get the Lipans drunk on alcohol, so they could take advantage of them in trade agreements. When the Indians sobered up and realized the situation, they left the missions for good. In the 1700s, the Lipan's biggest foe was the Mescalero tribe. Since the Lipans spent a lot of their time in the New Mexico Territory, they ran into the Mescalero quite often. The two tribes – Lipan and Mescalero - fought each other so much that the Lipan tribe actually begged the Spaniards to fight on their side and help them get an advantage over their enemy. The Spanish soldiers lined up with the Lipans in a few battles, but since the two groups didn't always see eye-to-eye, the alliance soon fell apart.

When the Mexicans ran the Spanish out of Mexico, they took back their government in 1821. Chief Flacco thought it would help his tribe, the Lipan, if he was friendly with the conquering Mexican government, so he traveled to Monclova, Coahuila. In that town, he met Gaspar Lopez and signed a peace treaty with this representative of the Mexican government. It seemed that Flacco tried diplomacy in dealing with the many governments that wanted to own Texas.

And the Mexicans definitely wanted to be a strong presence in Texas. They set up a religion that all Texas settlers had to abide by – the Catholic Church. The set of laws dictated by the

Mexican government wasn't what the white people flowing into Texas wanted to obey. As the years went by, the white settlers in Texas decided to fight for their independence from Mexico. As Sam Houston organized his fledging army to defend Texas, he had some Indian assistance. Chief Flacco of the Lipans was a close friend of Sam Houston. He received paying commissions in the newly formed Republic of Texas Army. Chief Flacco was a part of the Lower Rio Grande division of the Lipans, so he and his men fought for Texas Independence while the Upper division of the Lipans sided with Mexico.

Another white man who Chief Flacco knew well was Noah Smithwick. Noah came to Texas in 1827. He was a blacksmith and served as an interpreter agent with the Plains Indians when they were seeking treaties or doing business with the local trading posts. In Smithwick's book, *The Evolution of a State*, he tells about fighting with the Lipans as allies. In 1839 a party of Lipan Indians was hunting along the San Gabriel River and discovered a camp of Comanche Indians. The Comanche teepees were about fifty miles from Austin. The hunters knew they couldn't fight the Comanche by themselves, so they retreated home to get help. They enlisted Noah Smithwick and other white men in the area. No militia troops were in this vicinity, so Smithwick got men from LaGrange and Bastrop to fight with the Lipans. Juan Castro was head Chief of the Lipans at this time because Chief Flacco was much older and not as active. Flacco's son was also in the group of Lipan fighters.

With about sixty men plus the Lipans, Smithwick headed toward the Comanche camp. Since it was winter, an unexpected storm of snow and sleet stopped the little army. They hid in a grove of trees for three days. It was so frigid that the men suffered terribly from the cold conditions, and some of the horses froze to death. When the weather finally warmed up, the men found the Comanche camp and attacked it just at sunrise. Smithwick said, "Our men rushed right into their lodges. The women and children screaming, dogs barking, men yelling and shooting, in a moment transformed the peaceful scene on which the day had just dawned into a pandemonium."

The two enemies fought, retreated, and then opened fire on each other again. Smithwick saw his men gaining ground and defeating the Comanche, so he thought they were winning.

Lipan Apache in 1857 drawn by Arthur Schott.

But one of the older Texans, Colonel Moore, stopped all hostilities and ordered a retreat. At the time this happened, most of the settlers thought they were defeating the

113

Comanches and that the Indians were retreating. Stopping the battle made the Lipan Chief Castro very disgusted. He decided to double back and steal the Comanche's horses since the shooting had slowed down. While Chief Castro was doing that, the Comanches had the same idea. They stole most of the white's men ponies, so Smithwick said the Lipans took off with quite a few stolen horses. That dilemma left Smithwick and the other settlers without a horse and 100 miles from home.

Chief Castro, Cuelgas de Castro, who fought with Smithwick was a Lipan born into the Sun Otter band in 1792. His family lived near San Antonio and the South Texas region. His father was Chief Josef Chiquito who was from a long line of Lipan chiefs. The Castro part of his name was given to him by Ramon de Castro, military commander of the northeastern Spanish frontier provinces from 1787 to 1892. Chief Castro was chief of the Sun Otter band, so when Mexico defeated the French in 1822, Castro signed treaties with the new government in Mexico City. He was offered land grants by this treaty. Chief Castro felt beholding to the Mexicans, so he served in the Mexican army as a lieutenant colonel and drew a salary from the Republic of Mexico. His band received gifts and food subsidies at Laredo through the year 1827.

Chief Castro and his people lived along the border near Laredo and were willing to serve with which ever army won the war. When the Texans won their independence, he wisely switched his allegiance. He helped to protect the Texans after they won their independence from Mexico in 1836. He and his son, John Castro, fought as an auxiliary troop in Texas militia battles with the Comanche especially. When he wasn't playing soldier, Castro might be hunting buffalo. In 1840, the Sun Otter band of Lipans lived near a village called Estacas, below Laredo, Texas. Residents of that area remember Chief Castro bringing meat and skins to trade with the Mexicans. Chief Castro was quite unique because he owned a pet buffalo cow. Chief Castro made an interesting site when the buffalo cow followed behind him as he rode his horse. The cow turned heads.

Indian camp where meat was dried on racks to use later. Photo taken by William S. Soule in 1870. Courtesy of U. S. National Archives.

After the Lipans became friends with the Texans, they were used as scouts. Chief Flacco received some fame when he rode with the Texas Ranger named John "Jack" Coffee Hays. Jack admired Chief Flacco, and once he described him as "tall and erect, with well shaped limbs. He gave an impression of bounding elasticity. His circlet of eagle feathers was set back on his forehead so that it revealed his black eyes and gave to his bearing fierce alertness coupled with strength and agility." Hays said that Chief Flacco saved his life several times when they were fighting the Comanche, but Flacco said that a number of times, Hays saved his life also.

Even when the settlers began to turn against all the Indians, Chief Flacco and other Lipan chiefs such as Chief Castro continued to help the Texas government. In 1841, the two chiefs were arrested in Austin on the suspicion that one of their warriors had killed a settler named James Boyce. Both men said they didn't do it, but they were held in confinement until proof surfaced that Comanche warriors did the killing, not the Lipans. In spite of treatment like this, the Lipans continued to be friendly with the white settlers.

Flacco's younger son was loved by his father as well as the entire Lipan tribe. As soon as he was old enough to fight, he had taken the white man's side of the battles. After serving in many fights over a period of time, the Texas government realized the Young Flacco had done many brave deeds for them. They honored his heroics by giving Young Flacco a full colonel's uniform. A department clerk in the army also taught Young Flacco to write his name, but when he signed it, he followed the Spanish rule by placing the adjective after the noun- Flacco Colonel.

He and other Lipan warriors scouted and fought for General Somervell when his troops repelled the Mexicans troops who had crossed the Rio Grande in 1842. Flacco the Younger was at Goliad and helped drive the Mexicans back across the Rio Grande. Flacco had a friend who was a deaf mute, but he was a very good tracker, so he had helped on this maneuver. When Flacco and his companions started back to their home, the deaf mute became sick. He and Flacco stopped on the Medina River while the rest of the warriors continued homeward. While camping alone on the river, somebody killed the two Indians. Young Flacco's horses were seen in Sequin a few days later in the hands of Tom Thernon, and most observers knew what happened. But they didn't dare tell old Flacco the truth.

The older Flacco was very worried when his son did not return with the other warriors who went to the Rio Grande, so he and his wife visited Noah Smithwick to find out what happened. When they showed up at Noah's house, he wasn't surprised because Flacco had often brought them some game he had killed or brought a present like moccasins for Noah's little boy. But this time when the older couple came to his door, Noah knew something was wrong. The two Indians acted so worried that Noah sensed all was not well. He gave them something to eat and heard their story.

Smithwick didn't tell them what he had heard about their son's death. Instead he followed their request and wrote a letter to President Houston and General Burleson inquiring about what happened to their son. When Smithwick received the letters saying that Mexicans robbed and killed their son, he went to their camp and told them the sad story. Old Chief Flacco had been in many battles and had always showed no signs of weakness, but Noah Smithwick said that when he told him that his son was dead, he cried sobs that shook his aged body. Smithwick didn't dare tell any of the Indians that white men actually killed Young Flacco because he knew such news would start a war for sure.

After Flacco came to grips with the death of his son, he told Smithwick he wanted to give away everything that belonged to his son. The old man explained his actions by saying, "It has always been our custom to destroy everything belonging to the dead, but my son was the white man's friend and I want to do with his things as white men do." Chief Flacco gave four horses to Smithwick, a mare and a colt to General Burleson, and a young mustang that Young Flacco had trained went to Sam Houston. A while after Chief Flacco gave away his son's possessions, he and his small band of about 60 warriors headed toward the Rio Grande to find a new home.

Since Chief Flacco was a friend of Sam Houston, before he left Texas, Chief Flacco asked Houston to find the person who killed his son. Houston tried to pen the murder on Mexican bandits or on some Cherokee, but he never told Flacco that two white men were known to have done the job. When older Flacco died in about 1850, the two divisions of Lipans merged and fought as one Upper division.

Some tribes such as the Lipans gave the Mexican government so much trouble, that the new leaders decided the Lipans had to leave Coahuila. Once the Mexican government decided it was a good idea to eliminate the Lipans, they mounted a determined assault on them.

Sam Houston was a good friend of many Texas Indians including Chief Flacco.
Courtesy of the West Texas Collection, Angelo State University.

In 1869, Mexican troops came from Monterrey to fight the Indians at Zaragosa. The Mexican soldiers successfully demolished many Lipan camps. With so many Lipans dead, the survivors fled to the Mescaleros' camp. It has often been said that war makes strange bed fellows, and it was so with the alliance between the Lipan and the Mescaleros. Years before they had been fighting each other, and now they were living close together in Chihushua, Mexico and in New Mexico.

By 1879, there were few Lipan Indians in Texas. Their numbers dropped like the Tonkawa, and the Lipans found themselves living near Fort Griffin with the Tonkawa remnant. In 1884, the 17 Lipans living there were taken to Oklahoma to live on a reservation. In 1905, the census could only count 35 Lipans living, and ten of them were in Oklahoma. In more modern times, the Lipan have thirty members of their tribe in Oklahoma in 1951. Renewed interest in the tribe has occurred as a group has developed the Lipan Apache Museum in Corpus Christi, Texas in the Sunrise Mall.

Grinding holes such as these are remembrances of the Indian tribes who once lived Texas. Author's collection.

Mescalero Apache Chief, San Quan. Courtesy of U.S. National Archives.

Ch. 7 Comancheros

"The countryside wasn't fit for man or beast." Until progress brought windmills to the High Plains of Texas, this area was definitely unfit for permanent residence. The flat land had little protection from high wind and blizzards, and in the summer, the grass dried and the water disappeared from the streams. Visitors didn't see trees, hills, shelter, or much water. This area, sometimes called the Llano Estacado, was an area a traveler passed through, but didn't stay.

But this bleak area held an attraction for both the Indian and the Mexican. The practice of trading brought these two groups of human beings together in an unusual way in the 1800s. The Mexican traders, called Comancheros, dealt with a variety of different Indian tribes The bartering began in a small way because both Mexican and Indian walked everywhere they went.

When Indians pulled their belongings across the Texas plains using dogs, they didn't cover a very large section of the dusty ground called Llano Estacado. This part of the Texas Panhandle was bordered on the north by the Canadian River, on the west by the Mescalero Escarpment, on the south by the Edwards Plateau, and on the east by the Cap rock Escarpment. When trying to imagine how this country was situated, think of a high mesa that slopes about 10 feet per mile toward the southeast. This mesa is one of the largest tablelands on the continent. The Llano Estacado is about 200 miles long and 130 miles wide.

Indians had very little opportunity to trade for goods unless they came upon another tribe walking in that vicinity. Likewise, the Mexican trader walked and used a two-wheeled cart by which he could pull his few trade items. If he was lucky, he chanced upon an Indian camp and traded an item or two. But after the warriors acquired ponies, the Texas Indians had an ongoing trade agreement with the Mexicans who called themselves Comancheros. The Plains Indians got along quite well with the Mexicans during the time that Mexico possessed Texas. If the Mexican trader and the Indian customer met on the Texas plains, much bartering, eating and playing games took place.

Carreta, a kind of vehicle produced by Spanish-speaking people for centuries (from a Spanish colonial exhibit at the New Mexico Farm & Ranch Heritage Museum, Las Cruces, New Mexico).

Horses came to the Indians in an unusual way. According to W. W. Newcomb in *The Indians of Texas,* these people didn't own horses until after the settling of New Mexico. When Don Juan de Onate rode into Mexico in 1598, he brought about seven thousand animals with him. This future governor of the colony called New Mexico had three hundred mares and colts included in his livestock. As time passed, villages sprung up in the surrounding area, and Indians were employed or forced to take care of the Spaniard's horses. Although these warriors hated the treatment they received as slaves, through this arrangement, Indians learned a lot about the four-legged creatures.

Some of the men who were Spanish slaves escaped from their owners, and when they did, they took their knowledge of horses with them. A few Indians took more than know-how with them; they also stole horses for their own use. Apache tribes were numerous in that area, and they eventually stole enough horses that they could make raids on the outlying ranches. The revolt of the Pueblo Indians in 1680 brought more opportunities for the Indians. They took with them sheep, cattle, and horses that had previously been in the possession of Spanish settlers.

The Indians also learned from their captors how to make saddles. They stretched green buffalo hides over wooden frames. When the hide shrank, they tightened over the framework. Other Indians were seen using a stuffed pad to ride on. These pads usually had stirrups attached. Since Indians wanted to ride in battle with their bodies protected, they devised a rope loop on one side of the horse. They could suspend their bodies through this loop and ride hidden from their enemies.

The advent of horses on the Llano Estacado brought a variety of tribes there to trade with the Comancheros. If Apaches could ride horses, it was obvious to the Comanches that they could also. From the time the Comanches fastened their eyes on Spanish horses, they strove to replace their dog transports with these majestic beasts. Their first successful raids for horses were in 1719 in New Mexico. With horses they moved quickly to dominate both the Texas Panhandle as well as Central Texas by 1730. After warring with other tribes, they settled in the Staked Plains of the Texas Panhandle by 1750.

Before the plains Indians had horses, they lived off of their gardens as well as the Buffalo. Their villages were near a stream, and they did some type of irrigation for many years. But with the advent of the horse, Comanches became mobile. No longer did they dig the ditches and other backbreaking chores connected with irrigated fields.

Texas soon had another important Indian tribe move to Texas: it was the Kiowa. After 1763 the Lakota Sioux moved westward from Minnesota and settled in the Black Hills. They ran the Kiowa out of the Black Hills and claimed them as their own. The Kiowa were forced to find another homeland, so they traveled south. At first the Comanche attacked the Kiowa. One time in 1805, a group of Kiowa and Comanche braves were about to fight each other at a Spanish Trading Post. The trader nervously tried to keep the two groups apart. One Kiowa warrior volunteered to stay with the Comanches if they wouldn't fight. He stayed all summer and returned to his people as the leaves turned yellow in the fall. When the Kiowas saw him unharmed, they made peace with the Comanche and the tribes understood each other better after that experience.

Comanches had to find buffalo or other meat to eat because they weren't a farming tribe. They either bartered for what they needed or went on many buffalo hunts. They needed the hides when they reached their prime, so other hunts were planned in the fall months as related in *Indians of Texas* by W. W. Newcomb, Jr. According to Newcomb, the Comanches camped near available water and wood before a big Buffalo hunt was planned. The women worked hard in preparing the hides and meat after the warriors had successfully downed many Bison. Indians killed the buffalo either by piercing the animal's heart with an arrow or by driving a lance deep into his chest. Some of this meat was traded to the Comancheros..

Also the Comanches survived on other food they picked. Some of these foods could be traded also. During the growing season, they collected plums, grapes, juniper berries, mulberries, persimmons and the fruit of the prickly pear, tuna. Some roots were eaten as well as nuts such as pecans and acorns. On the Llano Estacada, Comanches also hunted deer and antelope. Texas did have their black bear in the early 1800s, so the Comanches killed them in the Cross Timbers region.

Shortly after 1786, the Spanish New Mexico government signed a treaty with the Comanche Indians. Juan Bautista de Anza started a policy that allowed New Mexican traders, Comancheros, to ride out on the plains and trade with the Comanches. The Comanches agreed to stop raiding in exchange for trade and gifts. According to Evetts Haley in *The Comanchero Trade,* the New Mexico traders were eager to reopen lines of trade that Spanish-Comanche wars had stopped. Juan Bautista de Anza encouraged this bartering because he felt there would be a profit for the traders. He also thought peaceful relations with the Plains tribes would prevent so many raids on the New Mexican communities. The traders from the Santa Fe area particularly liked to trade along the Llano Estacado.

The Comancheros loaded their carts or donkeys with beads, calico, tobacco, coffee, sugar, kettles and large knives. The Mexicans also loaded sacks of hard-baked cornbread onto their carts because the Indians really favored it. The Indians traded them horses, dried meat, hides, tallow, and captives in return. The Comancheros never had more than $20 of value in their carts because they never knew if and when they would find a band of Indians. Sometimes the Spanish government encouraged their trade, and at other times, they were hard on the Comancheros because they thought the trading encouraged the Comanches to steal more horses, which was probably true.

Even though trade was going well, after a period of time another change in government put the trading area under different management. By 1821 the Mexican government replaced the Spanish law in Texas, so the Indians had to deal with a new group of people ruling Texas. In 1822 and in 1826, Mexico made a treaty with a band of Comanches, but didn't keep it. However, Mexican peddlers did like to trade with the Comanches, and they were fair enough in their dealings, so they continued to seek the Indians on the plains. When dealings changed in New Mexico, the Comanches continued to raid livestock and captives. Captives were important because young male captors could grow up to be warriors and increase the size of the tribe. Female captives could be bartered for goods or taught to process meat and buffalo hides. This act added to the value of the tribe. The more women an Indian had in his possession, the more hides he would have to barter.

In this trading relationship, the Comanches became the suppliers of horses and buffalo hides. They obtained these by treaties, truces, and mutual understanding between the men on the high Plains. While the Comanches kept their peace with the New Mexicans, they could receive slaves and horses from Mexico and Texas.

According to Jay W. Sharp in "The Comanchero Trade and Trails", the main trails followed by the Comancheros began at Santa Fe, New Mexico and ran southeastward to the Pecos River, then downstream in the area where Fort Sumner is in Eastern Central New, Mexico. From there the trail ran east, southeast for 75 miles and then into Texas. It crossed the Texas cap rock and ended up in Ransom Canyon near present day Lubbock. Another trail went eastward across the High Plains and descended the eastern escarpment to a place near the present community of Quitaque, Texas.

The Indians preferred that the trading take place in a sheltered place, somewhere off the naked, windswept plains. Ransom Canyon was a good meeting place and Quitaque gave another type of protection. The Los Lingos stream in this region had cottonwood trees, willows and hackberries to protect the traders from the cold wind or blistering heat of summertime.

The High Plains were a special place where most of the trails were carved out in straight lines so the Comancheros and Indians could travel in the shortest line from one point to another. Smooth trails were also important, and with the help of satellite images, old Indian trails can still be seen from the air as they cut a deep groove in the disturbed sod.

As the years went by, the trading became more elaborate. The traders and Indians met at designated places, usually where there were springs and irrigation ditches watering crops. Some of these places were Los Lingo Creek, Pease

River, and Yellow House Canyon near present-day Lubbock. When bartering at these locations started, they could take weeks. At first, goods and cattle were the big trade items, but as time went on, the trading changed. Later on firearms, ammunition, whiskey, and some manufactured products were exchanged. Comancheros and the Indians played games and had horse races as well as drinking parties that lasted a long time.

As cattle came into Texas, the Comancheros were smart enough to barter for cattle they could sell or butcher. Of course the Comanches had ways to confiscate what cows they wanted also. Officials in both the Spanish and the Mexican government knew the Comancheros were trading for stolen cattle. But the strange thing was that wealthy New Mexican merchants profited by the cattle trade, so they didn't prevent the Comancheros from buying these animals. The Comancheros became proficient in locating people in Arizona and New Mexico who had government beef contracts. These men readily purchased any cattle the Comancheros could provide. Indians had ways to manage the market also. When buffalo weren't available, they slipped around the herd of cattle when nobody was on watch and took what they wanted.

The Comancheros knew that the Indians liked to trade for whiskey, but the Mexicans feared for their life when the Comanche got drunk. The Mexicans' devised a plan so they could distribute the liquor and still stay alive when the trade was completed. After the cattle were traded to the Comancheros, the Indians didn't receive their liquor right away. During the trade, the whiskey might be ten miles away, hidden in a safe place. After the Mexicans drove their newly acquired herd two or three days, several of their men delivered the whiskey. This was a tricky procedure because the Indians looked forward to their drinks. After the alcohol was delivered, one Mexican Juan Trijillo said, "We rode for our lives." While the Comanches traded with the Comancheros, another group wanted to trade with them also. American traders ventured out on the Plains because they had a ready market for the many buffalo hides the Indians accumulated. The eastern markets would pay a good price for these hides. In turn the Comanches received more manufactured goods from the traders than they had before.

The Republic of Mexico figured into this bartering that was taking place on the plains of Texas. During the years the Republic of Texas existed, 1836 to 1845, the young Republic needed to receive the taxes on goods that changed hands on the Santa Fe Trail. The young government hadn't devised a way to tax this commerce, so officials in Texas were upset.

Sand dunes such as those near modern day Monahans made traveling very hard for the Comancheros in this region, so they tried to travel on compact soil most of the trip across the plains.

Mexican traders were receiving the cash that the young government needed in Texas. According to Troy Ainsworth in "The Second Santa Fe Expedition: Jacob Snively and the Mission to Disrupt New Mexico Commerce in 1843," President Sam Houston authorized Jacob Snively to lead an expedition against the Mexican traders along the Santa Fe Trail.

The Republic of Texas had many financial woes. During their first six years of existence, they had a deficit of $5,783,429. They knew from observation that the amount of goods hauled over the Santa Fe Trail in one year was nearly a tenth of their deficit. Snively was to attack the traders and seize their cargo. Half of their booty would go to the government and half to the men on the Expedition. This idea certainly sounded good to Snively.

The group of about one-hundred sixty men left Fort Johnson on the Red River on April 25, 1843. The men traveled through the present-day counties of Grayson, Cooke, Montague, Clay and Wichita, crossed the Red River, and continued through Oklahoma to Kansas. The Arkansas River was the northern boundary of Texas at that time. After three weeks of searching for the Mexican Caravans, Snively's group finally located some Mexicans. But they were a military attachment who was in the area to protect the Mexican traders. The fact that they weren't traders didn't seem to make any difference to the soldiers. Snively was ready for a fight, so he led his troops against them. The battle was one-sided, so the Texans did well by killing seventeen Mexicans while not losing a single soldier.

The Texans won, but received very little treasure from the 82 soldiers that they captured. After holding the prisoners for eight days, the Texans were discouraged and bored. They released the prisoners and divided the spoils of a few mules, some tack, and saddles. Snively thought about disorganizing the expedition, but they weren't home yet. Two days later they were confronted by Captain Cooke and his U.S. dragoons. Cooke actually believed that the Texans were on U.S. soil, and he disarmed the whole group, and wrote in his report that he thought they were a bunch of bandits. Captain Cooke did ask Snively's men if they wanted to go with his forces back to safety, but no one took him up on the offer.

So when Snively's Texans crossed the Cimarron River a few days later, they were nearly all ready to quit the expedition. They officially disbanded at a point between present-day Fort Worth and Dallas. The arguments continued, though, between the Texans and Captain Cooke. The Texans filed a complaint for restitution of their property that Captain Cooke had taken. Three years later on July 14, 1846, Congress of the United

States granted each member of Snively's Expedition $18.75 for weapons taken from them. From that point on, Texas didn't try to bother the Mexican traders anymore.

Trading was brisk between the Indians and the Comancheros. All was going well for both sides of the trading relationship until the drought started in the last half of 1840. Water became a precious commodity as more streams and springs dried up. The Plains tribes couldn't get enough buffalo hides to trade for things they needed such as corn, guns, and other things they were used to having in their lodges. The drought continued into the 1850s. Normally the Plains Indians would have migrated east to find buffalo and food, but misplaced eastern tribes made the movement of the Plains tribes difficult. This was a case of too many people trying to live off of too little.

The Plains Indians were forced to stay on the Llano Estacado where there was little grass or water. Occasionally the hungry Indians had to go to war to obtain food and supplies. At other times, they relied on the United States government to help them more than they ever had before. J. W. Whitefield was appointed to oversee the Upper Arkansas Indian Agency. He reported to the Secretary of State in his *Report of the Commissioner of Indian Affairs in 1854 and 1855* that Indians had begun to stop passing wagons and beg for coffee, sugar, and other items for which they normally traded. The situation got so bad that eventually the Indians ate their horses and mules.

One Comanche chief, Tibbalo, asked his neighbors to intercede on his behalf. He said, "There were 5,000 of his tribe in a destitute condition." They were camped along the Arkansas River, and he asked for some land between it and the Red River, land he had signed away in a treaty but needed now. Some Penateka Comanches took up residence on the 2,000 acre Clear Fork Reservation, but other bands continued to go on raiding parties. They wanted to raid into Mexico but the U. S. stopped that. Then they began raiding on the U.S. side of the Rio Grande. Finally Reservation Indians were allowed to hunt outside of the reserve because if the government didn't let them, they would starve.

The trade between the Comancheros and the Indians lasted a long time. Even though the Mexican government was in chaos at times, the trading continued. More settlers came to Texas, but trading continued. The greatest amount of bartering between the Mexicans and the Indians took place during the Civil War, and reached its peak during those years. Firearms, whiskey, and slaves were exchanged. There was little defense on the Plains during the war days, so Comanche warriors stole Confederate livestock and sold them to the Comancheros. The Mexicans turned around and sold the cattle to the Union agents. Only the presence of the U. S. Army finally stopped the trading when the Civil War was over and soldiers came back to occupy the forts in Texas.

Just because the war was over, it didn't stop the swapping of goods though. In the 1860s the Comanche continued to trade with the Comancheros because the Comanche refused to live on the reservation assigned to them in 1867. This was a good time for the Comancheros too because men such as Jose P. Tafoya made enough money from trading to invest in sheep, cattle ranching and freighting.

While the Comancheros were traveling in small groups across the plains with their carts or wagons, sometimes a large group of one hundred or more Mexican men were seen hunting buffalo. They sometimes brought their wives and children and camped for many days preparing the meat for winter use. These people weren't interested in trade. They were called Ciboleros as they rode their Spanish ponies and used bows and arrows or lances to kill the buffalo. Some excellent hunters could kill twenty-five buffalo during a single chase. Wives and children scraped the hides and prepared the meat after the Buffalo were shot. They stayed behind to work while the hunters moved to a different location. A mixture of buffalo brains was rubbed on the clean skin-side of the hide to tan and preserve it. Most of the meat was made into jerky. At the kill site, they heated the fat into tallow. The children liked to watch the big hunks of fat change to tallow because a surprise was coming. After the tallow was removed, the crunchy cracklings were given to the children as a treat. The Ciboleros used just about all parts of the buffalo for something. Their hides made warm robes or rugs for their tents in the winter. Buffalo horns made utensils or decorative objects.

Although the Ciboleros didn't want to have anything to do with the Indians, they came on their hunt prepared for a battle or bartering, which ever was necessary. If the Comanche came to their camp, the Mexicans had homemade bread, beads, and other trinkets to barter with the Indians. If an Indian hunting party came by the Cibolo camp, the Mexicans might give them flour, sugar, or coffee. The Ciboleros wanted to stay on the good side of the Indians because both parties were dependent upon the buffalo.

Most of the Ciboleros lived along the Rio Grande. When they returned to their villages with the products of a successful hunt, the whole village celebrated. Usually the town threw a party for the hunters after they came home. Eventually most of the meat was sold to the villagers except for the amount the hunter's family needed. Much of the meat and products from the hunt were sold in New Mexico or northern Mexico.

As early as 1832, the Ciboleros were believed to have killed as many as 10,000 to 12,000 bison each year. They made a big dent in the Indians' meat supply as the years went by. Just as white men were accused of killing the buffalo for its tongue, the Ciboleros did also. They shipped the delicacy as far south as Mexico City where one dried tongue brought as much as two dollars. Historians think the Ciboleros encouraged the Comanchero trade to start when they told of their success on the plains of Texas. By the 1850s, the Comanches were not pleased with the Ciboleros success in killing buffalo. The Indians warned the Mexican hunters to bring only a few pack mules to take back their meat rather than a large wagon. After the Civil War, the U.S. troops tried to stop the Ciboleros hunting parties as the troops fought the Indians, but the Mexican hunters were sly. They knew the trails well and avoided the soldiers. They continued to hunt the buffalo until they were completely gone in the 1870s. The Comanches were forced to live on reservations much to their sorrow.

Buffalo hunters at their camp in Texas, about 1877.

A combination of buffalo hunters almost wiped out the buffalo so that few small herds were left. In modern times, some ranchers have slowly brought the great animals back from extinction. As a result, buffalo meat is considered a desirable entrée to order today because of its low fat content.

Cibolero ready to hunt Buffalo on the plains. Courtesy of the Encyclopedia of the Great Plains.

Ch. 8 Comanches

Of all the Indian tribes known in America, probably the Comanche were the most militant but still the most colorful in their personality. In spite of their aggressive nature, they did show their human side as they dealt with some Texans. Before their sojourn in Texas, they had first been part of the Eastern Shoshone near Wind River in far away Wyoming. But they broke away from them in 1500. With dogs for transport, their hunting trips were somewhat limited in distance as they searched for the Buffalo. Nearly two hundred years later the Comanche obtained horses as a result of the 1680 Pueblo Rebellion.

In the next twenty years, their journeys brought them to New Mexico as they traded with the Utes at the Taos pueblos. Now the Comanche and his horse were a force to be reckoned with as they swept across the plains. Several tribes fought together when the Spanish soldiers attacked them in 1716 in Northern New Mexico. Sadly some of the Indians were captured by the Spanish and later sold as slaves.

Through the wars against the Spanish and against the Apaches, the Comanche ruled the Texas Plains by 1730. They were able to buy firearms from the French traders, so their alliance with any band or tribe was now not necessary. They dropped their alliance with the Utes and fought them as much as the Apaches or the Spanish. As they received more horses and arms, their power was stronger than ever. They made and broke treaties often. This behavior continued into the 1800s.

But something unusual happened in 1807 and 1808. The Comanche warriors were seen wearing red jackets, a most unusual attire for them. This story was found in Federal Indian Agent Dr. John Sibley's report from a meeting that was held in 1807 at Natchitoches, Louisiana. This encounter that Sibley had with the Comanches took place at a frontier fort on the Red River. He had money to buy gifts for the visiting Indians, so he described in his report that 80 Comanches, along with four chiefs came to trade. He gave all the Indians some provisions, cooking utensils, and tobacco, but the chiefs received special gifts.

He gave them each a hat, plume, calico shirt, parcels of paint, britch clouts, looking glasses, knives, black silk handkerchiefs, and combs. That day, August 11, 1807, Sibley invited the four chiefs to his house. He entertained them, smoked with them, and offered them spirits, but they refused. Then Dr. Sibley sent for a tailor and had each of them measured for a scarlet coat faced with black velvet and trimmed with white buttons.

Nearly a year later, the red coats appeared once more worn by Comanche Indians. This time Captain Don Francisco Amangual was commanding about 200 Spanish soldiers who left San Antonio de Bexar on March 30, 1808 with plans to reach Santa Fe, New Mexico. Francisco rode to the San Saba River with the intention of seeing the ruins of Presidio of San Luis dela Amarillas, near present day Menard. At the ruins, they met two Comanche from the nearby Rancheria of a Chief called Cordero. They visited him and his tribe for several days until they continued on toward the land of several rivers. From this green area, probably the Conchos, they rode through red hills and a red river, probably the Colorado River. The red soil had a way of changing the color of the water.

At this point in their trip, they saw a small group of Indians who invited them to come to their Rancheria nearby. Comanche Chief Isambanbi visited the Spanish soldiers and stayed in their camp the first night. Before Isambanbi left camp the next day, he invited Capt. Francisco Amangual to visit his home the following day. The day the Spaniards rode into the Comanche camp, May 8, 1808, they received a cordial but unusual greeting. Capt. Amangual said, "Upon our arrival the big chief and the other chiefs of the tribe came out to meet us. They were very well dressed, but they wore very unusual clothes: very long red coats, with blue collars and cuffs, white buttons, yellow imitation gold galloon; and one of them was dressed in ancient Spanish style; a short red coat, blue trousers, white stockings, English spurs, an ordinary hat worn cocked, and a cane with a silver handle shaped like a hyssop." Although they were quite elegantly dressed, they painted their faces with chalk and red ochre, and their nicely braided hair trailed to the ground. Although no one was sure, these Indians must have been the same ones who received coats from Agent Sibley about seven months before.

But the beautiful coats didn't keep them from going on the warpath from time to time. The various Comanche bands had warred with just about everyone in Texas. They didn't get along with other Indian tribes or the Mexican government or the white settlers. As the years went by, the army could police the Rio Grande better, so the Comanche didn't go on raids into Mexico as much as they previously had.

During the 1830s, more attempts were made to have peace negotiations with the Indians in Texas. In 1833, Sam Houston talked peace with the Comanche and became friends with many of them in Texas. He had married an Indian widow when he lived with the Cherokee, so it was easy for him to speak to the Comanche. He gave the Indians a medal of President Jackson and instructed them to give it to their principal chief. Houston also wrote Jackson about the meeting and felt that the Comanche would adhere to the agreement

While Texas fought for its freedom from the Mexicans, the Comanche remained pretty well neutral. They had to be impressed at the fighting ability of the Texans, because they talked peace with more earnestness in their voices after Texas won their independence. Maybe Houston's effort to stay on friendly terms with the Indians had some effect also. In 1838 one hundred and fifty Comanche met in San Antonio and asked that a peace delegation meet with them. The Texans met the Indians and talked with them, but the Comanche had an important demand in their peace talk. They wanted a permanent boundary line be drawn between them and the huge number of settlers who were coming over their prairies. The group of men in San Antonio had no power to form such a boundary, so the talks died. In the spring, they had another council, and this time General Albert Sidney Johnston talked with them. He made it clear that there would be no boundary clause. The Comanche knew that the settlers would continue to spill over onto their hunting grounds, and there was nothing short of war that they could do to stop them.

Even so, during the winter of 1839-40, some southern Comanche asked for peace and wanted to have a council with the white men. Many of their people believed that the white settlers would eventually control the land, so they wanted to talk to the white leaders in their area. In the spring of 1840, the Comanche were invited to San Antonio to parley. Sixty-five Indians, including men, women, and children, came to the courthouse in San Antonio to talk peace.

The men went inside to talk while the women and children stayed outside. One of the conditions of the meeting had been for the Comanche to bring their prisoners to the council. They brought only one white captive to the meeting. When the soldiers saw only one captive, they must have thought something wasn't right because they took all the Indians into custody. This particular band of Indians may have had only one captive at the time, but they weren't allowed time to explain. The troops opened fire and thirty-five Indians were killed. Some of the slain were women and children. Seven white persons were killed and eight wounded. The Indians felt there was great deception by the white soldiers at the San Antonio Courthouse Battle, so it didn't take long to spread the word that an important war council would take place. The smoke signalers must have worked overtime getting the "word" out to all the Comanche bands. Many Comanche warriors were ready to go on the warpath.

When the other Comanche bands found out about San Antonio, they tortured their prisoners and killed thirteen in all. Retaliation time was at hand, so it wasn't surprising that Chief Buffalo Hump directed his warriors on a thousand mile raid in Texas where many homes were burned and settlers killed.

Buffalo Hump and other Comanche braves and their families numbered close to 1,000 when they appeared in Victoria August 6, 1840, without warning. John J. Linn saw the attack first hand and later wrote, "We of Victoria were startled by the apparitions presented by the sudden appearance of six hundred mounted Comanche in the immediate outskirts of the village." In John's book, *Reminiscences of Fifty Years in Texas*, he said the Comanche killed quite a few slaves working in the fields and white people who couldn't make it into town to safety. Some Mexican traders had been in Victoria selling horses that day, so the Indians captured their ponies as well as those belonging to local citizens. When the Indians left town with the horses, someone estimated that they had snatched about 1,500 ponies in all.

Surprisingly the town of Victoria was defended well enough that the Indians didn't really sack it like they planned to. As the fighting slowed down and the day ended, the Indians camped along the Placido or Placedo Creek. At this stop they were about 12 miles from Linnville, their next target. On the road to Linnville, they killed one wagon driver while another man escaped. Linnville had two people who told them an attack was eminent. Daniel D. Brown warned the citizens of danger and Mary Margaret Kerr Mitchell rode horseback across Prairie Chicken Reef to tell Victoria's fate.

In spite of all this warning, when the Comanche came to Linnville two days after attacking Victoria, most people thought they were Mexican horse traders. The Comanche surrounded the little town and destroyed stores and houses. The Indians killed three white people including customs officer Hugh Oran Watts. He returned to his house to retrieve a gold watch instead of escaping when he could. His wife, Juliet Constance, and a black woman with her child were captured by the Indians.

Most of the people running to safety ran into the water of the bay. They got on small boats and rowed out into the deeper water or they got on board a schooner, which was captained by William G. Marshall. The Comanche didn't venture into the water, so the townspeople got a good view of the ransacking of the rest of the town. A waterfront view, as it were.

They watched in horror as the Comanche torched buildings or plundered others. Some Indians tied bolts of cloth or feather beds to their horses and pulled them about town. When they discovered cattle running loose, the Indians rounded them up in a pen and slaughtered them. One man on the boats, Judge John Hays, couldn't stand to see the carnage, so he took his gun and waded to shore. The Indians didn't pay him any attention. When he later climbed back in the boat, Judge Hays found that it was a good thing he didn't try to fire on anybody because he didn't have any bullets in his gun.

The Indians tore open merchandise that was intended to go from New Orleans to San Antonio. In one warehouse, the Indians opened cases of umbrellas and hats that were bound for James Robinson's store in San Antonio. Observers watched the Indians playing with their loot and remarked, "These the Indians made free with, and went dashing about the blazing village, amid their screeching squaws and 'little injuns,' like demons in a drunken saturnalia, with Robinson's hats on their heads and Robinson's umbrellas bobbing about on every side like tipsy young balloons."

After the Indians tired of celebration, they loaded their new toys onto their mules, circled the 3,000 horses they had, and drove them to their camp across the road near the bayou. Their prisoner, Mrs. Juliet Watts, also made it to camp. While the Indians rested, the settlers were accumulating help from several points.

The men of Victoria collected volunteers from the Cuero Creek settlement. This group, along with volunteers from Gonzales and Lavaca formed a small army under the guidance of Adam Zumwalt and Benjamin McColloch. Their first skirmish with the Indians was about 12 miles east of Victoria on Mercado Creek. Later they fought at Casa Blanca Creek. At neither of these battles could the settlers liberate the prisoners, but the white men didn't quit. They followed the Indians and added to their forces until they met the Comanche again at Plum Creek.

The warriors were ready for another battle. Since the Comanche were 500 strong and had their ponies decorated for the battle, the Texans knew the Indians had prepared for this confrontation also. The warriors had stolen ribbons and fabric in their past conquests against the settlers and used them to decorate their horses. With their white shields catching the sunlight and the ribbons flowing from their horses, the Texas militia knew they were in for a battle.

When the Indians advanced against the Texas army, General Felix Huston led about 200 soldiers into the battle against them August 12, 1840. Huston was outmanned, but his troops fought the approaching warriors. After a few shots were fired, the Indians seemed to be disorganized. The troopers kept firing, and soon 30 to 40 Indians lay dead on the battleground. The Comanche warriors ran away, leaving the dead behind. Plum Creek was a surprising victory for the militia.

While the Plum Creek Battle between the Indians and the volunteers took place, the Indians tried to kill their captives. One prisoner, Juliet Watts, was shot with arrows like the other prisoners but her corset kept the arrows from killing her. Juliet returned to the Linnville area and eventually married Dr. J. M. Stanton. She later opened the Stanton House, which was the first hotel in Port Lavaca. Quite a few Linnville residents moved the 3 1\2 miles southwest of their former home to establish residence in Port Lavaca.

Some Tonkawa braves fought with the U.S. soldiers that day, and wanted to celebrate the victory. The American soldiers could hardly believe what happened after the battle. The Tonks dragged a dead Comanche warrior into their camp. They built a large fire, sliced pieces of the dead warrior off so they could spear it with a stick and cook it over the fire. The few soldiers who saw the incident were asked if they wanted a bite. They said, "No," while watching the cannibals with disgust. The Tonkawa ate the meat and began to dance and sing. They seemed to get drunk in their merriment as they continued to chant and sing until sunrise the next day.

There is reason to believe that this invasion along the Gulf of Mexico by the Comanche was part of a plan devised by Mexican Centralists to punish the citizens of Victoria and

Linnville for providing Mexican Federalists a port and site for the short-lived provisional government of the Republic of the Rio Grande. The captured plunder acquired by the Comanche showed up some time later as property of the Centralist Generals Valentin Canalizo and Adrian Wolf. These same horses were noticed as being owned by the Mexicans when they invaded Texas. Linnville as a town disappeared while Port Lavaca prospered.

To explain the Mexican Centralists, one has to understand Santa Anna's change in the way he governed. He was angry with some Mexican citizens, so he suspended the Mexican constitution and disbanded congress. He made himself the central power of Mexico. This action caused several uprisings, including the Texas Revolution.

Some of the leaders of the opposition had a meeting January 17, 1840 at the Orevena Ranch near Laredo. Men from Coahuila, Nuevo Leon, and Tamaulipa advocated rebellion and succession from Mexico. The rebels at the meeting wanted to form a federal republic with Laredo as capital, but they never got help from their states' congress and governments. No action was taken by the rebels.

With so much unrest along the border and with the Indians warring, Texas was in a turmoil. The state government knew they must protect the people, so the Texas Rangers were formed to fight primarily the Comanche. Treaties between the Republic of Texas and the Comanche were signed, but the Texans were afraid the Indians would break them at the least provocation.

The official Texas Rangers were organized in Texas at this time because the government had a lot of trouble controlling some Mexican groups and most of the Indian tribes. The Rangers were a group who traveled light and could strike at any place in the state without much notice ahead of time. They seldom had any type of uniform to wear so their identity was hard to recognize. That didn't seem to bother this unorthodox group whose only identity lay in the silver star they hung on their coat.

With the Rangers and other home militia groups watching the Indian's ever move, no one thought the Comanche would settle down. But in 1844, Sam Houston met with Chief Tseep Tasewah and other Indian leaders. The following year, 1845, a treaty was signed between the Republic of Texas and a Texas band of Comanche. Changes were happening fast as the United States annexed Texas in 1846, so some of the treaties made with the Texas government could have fallen by the wayside as the Indians argued that the Texas government treaties weren't relevant anymore. Luckily the Butler-Lewis Treaty of 1846 was made with the Comanche as well as the Anadarko, Caddo, Lipan, Wichita, and Waco. The Comanches did have a delegation who visited President Polk in 1846.

Little is said about any women signing these treaties, but "Kewiddawippa" signed the Butler-Lewis Treaty and she was a wife of Comanche war-chief Santa Anna. She was known to have accompanied her husband to visit President Polk after the signing of the treaty. Polk said in his journal dated July, 1846, "Among the Comanches and other wild Indians of the pra(i)ries were several women or squaws, and among others the wife of Santa Anna, the Comanche Chief was present."

Another person who mentioned Santa Anna's wife was with Mackenzie on his trip through Texas. William Parker made notes about his travels during the "Expedition Through Unexplored Texas" in the summer and fall of 1854. Parker told of an interesting Indian woman who went along with the expedition. He said she was the widow of Chief Santa Anna who died around 1851. This chief died of Cholera. Parker explained that she was still mourning her husband's death because in the evening she went outside the camp to wail and cut herself. At this time she had separated from her tribe and formed a small tribe of seven women who were all widows. He thought Kewiddawippa was doing well because she was an excellent hunter who had killed fifteen deer with her rifle in one morning. In describing her he said, "She was a fine looking woman, an Amazon in size and haughty bearing, rode astride, and dressed in deep black."

143

The famous Texas Ranger, Rip Ford, also met her. In September 24, 1850, he was camped at Los Ojuelos, Fort McIntosh, and he saw two Indian women coming to his camp. Rip had previously captured the Comanche prisoner, Carne Muerto, and one of these women was his mother. The other woman was the mother of another young brave, cousin of Carne Muerto, who Ford's men had killed at Benavides ranch. Ford knew they wanted to know the fate of their children, but he was very surprised that they had been able to travel such a distance without being harmed. The two women had passed between different military stations of regular soldiers as well as rangers without being detected, quite a fete.

The first men to speak to the Indian mothers were the interpreters who worked with the scouts. Warren Lyons and Roque were good interpreters, so they took the women to see Rip Ford. As Kewiddawippa looked into Ford's face and held his hand, tears fell from her eyes. Ford explained that Carne Muerto was being taken good care of and he explained the other boy had such a bad wound that he couldn't be saved so they "killed the Indian out of mercy." Ford emphasized the good treatment of the young Indians because he asked their mothers to explain this action to other Indians "in the event any of our people fell into the hands of the Comanche, to beg them to treat the unfortunates as we had her son."

The two Indian women stayed in the Laredo area for some time. They received many gifts from the people of the area and finally departed to return to their people.

Although the Butler-Lewis Treaty was made with the "Great White Father," many Texans didn't know how the Comanche would act once they were met in some village or on the open plains. Into this scenario came a German named John Meusebach who made a treaty with the Comanches in 1847 that still holds today. How did he do it? Maybe his early years at his home in Germany give a little clue as to how he could function so well in the wilds of Texas.

John was born May 26, 1812, at Dillenburg, Germany and was one of four children born to Baron Carl Hartwig Gregor von

Meusebach and Ernestine von Witzleban Meusebach. After going to the parochial school at Rossleben, he studied in the Mining and Forest Academy at Clausthal in the Harz Mountains. In 1832 he went to the University of Bonn and specialized in law. He added cameralism and finance as supporting fields. As if this variety of subjects didn't make him versatile enough, on the side he learned to speak five languages, including English. In 1836 he took his bar exams and began to work in administrative posts at Trier, Berlin, Potsdam, and other towns.

In 1845 John Meusebach's life took a drastic turn. The Society for the Protection of Immigrants in Texas appointed him commissioner general in Texas. This organization was called Adelsverein. They would pay John an annual salary of $790, but he would also received $2,000 with which he could purchase scientific equipment. He would also receive 2 percent of all net profits of the society and 500 acres of land. As educated a man as he was, Meusebach could surely have declined this job to be shipped to an uncivilized country. But he didn't.

After Meusebach sailed toward Texas, he arrived in the Gulf of Mexico in May of 1845. Since most of the German immigrants were at New Braunfels, some 165 miles away from the coast, he traveled directly to his post and saw a lot of his new home called Texas as he advanced westward. The scenery would have changed from the sand dunes of the coast to the flat lands, and then to small hilly country with little streams gurgling about.

Not long after he arrived in Texas, Meusebach was overrun by immigrants. Right away he realized that the government had sent too many immigrants to assimilate in such a short time. He needed more wagons to transport the new Texans than he had available.

Meusebach did realize that he had a large amount of land to make use of in the Fisher-Miller Land Grant. He wanted to survey the land grants so that families could move to their new homes, but he had one big obstacle: the Comanche Indians who lived in Central Texas. Scouting reports of the area suggested that the Comanche were on the warpath again.

John Meusebach, a German immigration leader, made a lasting treaty with the Comanche near Fredericksburg, Texas.

Even so, John used an Indian interpreter, Jim Shaw, and spoke to some Comanche in December of 1846.

John Meusebach was fortunate to have the services of guide, Jim Shaw. Jim was a Delaware Indian who could interpret as well as guide parties through unknown, unpopulated areas of Texas. He was first seen in Texas about 1841, when he was only twenty or thirty years old. With permission from the Spanish government, some Delaware tribes had previously crossed the Mississippi, traveled to Arkansas and made it to Texas by 1820. However, they didn't stay in Texas very long. When Houston needed scouts to calm the Indian problems in his second administration, he contacted former Governor Pierce Butler of South Carolina. Since Butler was the United States Indian agent among the Cherokees in the Indian Territory, he knew which men could do the job best. He sent Delaware scouts, Jim Shaw and John Conner. At an earlier time, Jim Shaw had avoided Texas governor Mirabeau Lamar because the governor disliked Indians so much, but he made himself available to Governor Pierce Butler a little later. Shaw was a handsome man who dressed and had manners much like the most cordial white man. One time German Ferdinand Roemer, who came to Texas with Meusebach, described what Shaw looked like from the rear.

Roemer said, "At the head of our party, on a beautiful American horse, rode our Delaware chief, Jim Shaw, a six-foot, handsome man. As one looked at him from the rear he had an entirely civilized appearance in his dark stylish coat, which he had purchased in a clothing store before leaving Austin, and his black, half-military, stiff-clothed cap. But as one looked at him from the front one observed the features and the brown skin of the Indian. Furthermore, one observed on close inspection that the European dress was not complete, for the leggings of deer-skin made up his dress below the coat."

This council with Comanche Indians wasn't new to Jim Shaw. In 1843, he accompanied Col. J. C. Eldridge, commissioner of Indian Affairs of the Republic of Texas and Hamilton P. Bee to speak to the Comanche. As they neared the Red River, Jim Shaw explained how he had observed the ill-fated Santa Fe Expedition that had passed through this area two years before. He explained that he watched them go up the Wichita River when they thought it was the Red River. Jim Shaw told Bee that he was riding alone, and he was afraid to go to the Expedition and tell them their error.

Delaware scout Jim Shaw also was an interpreter for an Indian Council at Bird's Fort, on the Trinity in the fall of 1843, and in December of that same year, he went with Pierce M Butler, United States Commissioner, to visit Pa-ha-eu-ka who was the head of the Comanche Nation. This chief was in no mood for Council because he was in mourning after losing his favorite son. It's a wonder the small treaty group got out of camp unharmed.

But the event Jim Shaw was most remembered for was the treaties he helped make between the Germans and the Comanche near present day Fredericksburg.

This bronze statue of John Meusebach and the Comanche are downtown Fredericksburg, Texas. Author's collection.

On this trip, the men liked to sing their well-known songs around the campfire at night. After they finished, Chief Shaw decided to add his version of music around the campfire also. He lay on his back and struck his abdomen with the palm of his hand to add rhythm to his music. The Germans didn't seem to appreciate this type of music as much as the Indians did.

As early as August of 1845, Jim Shaw guided Benjamin Sloat, the Texas Indian agent, to parlay with Buffalo Hump and other Penateka Comanche chiefs. Jim Shaw always tried to get along with other Indians, but one time he was in a Comanche camp when word came in the camp that Delaware Indians killed three Comanche warriors at Saint Mark a few months before. Suddenly Jim Shaw and his traveling companions found themselves being guarded at night for fear that some family member of the slain Indians would attack them. After holding council with the Comanche, Shaw asked them how he and his men could make restitution. Someone suggested that Jim's group give gifts to the chief to make amends. Jim didn't want to appear scared, so he began bargaining with the Indians. Finally he and Indian Agent Sloat got the Comanche to agree to settle the matter of the dead Comanche for the following gifts: "6 ½ yards of square cloth, 4 butcher knives, 4 papers of paint, looking glasses, 8 plugs of tobacco, 4 pounds of powder, 8 bars of lead, and 4 cotton handkerchiefs." Benjamin Shaw recorded this list of gifts in his report July 12, 1845 Indian papers 1844-1845.

Scout Jim Shaw had some unusual requests in his line of work. He was good friends with Comanche Chief Mope-cho-cope who was camped one time on the Colorado River above Austin. One of the chief's favorite wives ran away and he loved her, so he wanted her back. He sent word for Jim Shaw to try to find her and bring her back unharmed. He trusted this job to Jim rather than one of his own tribesman. One time influential Comanche Chief Buffalo Hump told Sam Houston that if he ever needed to confer with him, just send word through Jim Shaw.

For this reason, the Comanche were more receptive to visit John Meusebach than they would have been if Jim Shaw wasn't part of the peace plan.

After Meusebach visited the Indians in December of 1846, he asked if the Indians could meet with him later in the spring. They rendezvoused with him and Jim Shaw on the lower San Saba River in early March of 1847.

A group of German settlers traveled with Meusebach and met with ten Comanche chiefs including Buffalo Hump and Old Owl. The meeting took place at a settlement that John was credited as having founded, Fredericksburg. On May 9, 1847, the Comanche chiefs came to Fredericksburg and signed the Meusebach-Comanche Treaty. Chief Santa Anna also signed the treaty. They collected their gifts worth $3,000 and agreed to not bother the surveyors or the settlers. Considering all the turmoil the Comanche had brought to Texas settlers, it was surprising that the Comanche never broke that treaty they made with John Meusebach.

After several years, John Meusebach resigned from his job but continued to live near Fredericksburg and served as a Texas Senator in 1851. He retired with his wife to their 200 acre farm in Loyal Valley in 1869.

While Meusebach was dealing with Comanche near Fredericksburg, other Comanche bands were setting up camp in West Texas. The few settlers trying to ranch or farm in that area asked the government for protection from the Indian tribes who were raiding their homes. In 1852 the U.S. Army made their presence known in that uninhabited land. They decided to pitch their tents permanently on the North Concho River. Although there were pecan trees along the river, the land was flat and had little vegetation on it. This camp was called Camp Johnston and was named after surveyor Col. Joseph E. Johnston.

The Indians of the area got along quite well during the summertime because they could gather wild fruit and berries. But when the cold north wind blew across the countryside like a banshee, life for these Comanches wasn't so easy. When their supply of buffalo meat was used up, the Indians decided to move their teepees near Camp Johnston. As they begged for food, the Indians got to know the soldiers pretty well.

The commander of this camp, Capt. Arthur T. Lee, found opportunities to visit with the nearby Indians, and he got to know some of them quite well. Chief Yellow Wolf became friends with Capt. Lee. The Chief didn't know that this leader in an army uniform was really a painter. One day Capt. Lee convinced Chief Yellow Wolf to set for a painting. After several sessions of painting, the end result was a likeness that was quite good. Many years later Capt. Lee returned to the eastern states with his painting of Chief Yellow Wolf. This picture was later displayed in the Museum and Science Center of Rochester, New York.

Other Comanches camped at a special place, which is now called Santa Anna Peak, in Coleman County. Information about this encampment came largely from Emmor Harston, an adopted member of the tribe. Emmor's father was an Indian trader. He explained that Santa Anna's mother, Wap-so-ni, was the female governor of Conas, a warrior training camp at what is now called Santa Anna Peak. The town of Santa Anna has annual "Funtier Days" where they celebrate their history. Some descendants of the Comanche have returned to share their history also.

Bill Neely, the Comanche Tribal Historian recently wrote, "Texas is a religion. Our land is sacred to all races who live and have lived upon it. As we once fought for its possession, let us now pray together for our integration with it and our harmonious unity as we reflect upon a stormy past."

Santa Anna's Peak, where the Comanche camped in the 1800s, is actually twin peaks that are flat topped mesas about 300 feet high. They are a good lookout spot. The land around them is flat. Atop these mesas one can see fifty miles to the Salt Gap in the Brady Mountains, or forty miles to Caddo Peaks. This site is located in Coleman County, Texas and is north of the Colorado River and near the point where the Edwards Plateau, Llano Basin, and Cross Timbers meet.

Chief Santa Anna of the Comanches was at the height of his greatness during this time that he lived here. In the 1840s, Chief Santa Ann was busy signing treaties because he is known to have signed one with the Republic of Texas, the United States, and the German settlers at Fredericksburg. In1846, he was the first Comanche representative to visit "the White Father" in Washington.

According to the writings of J. Emmor Harston, son of an Indian trader, an eternal fire was kept burning on the top of the peaks because the Comanche used both fire and smoke for

Santa Anna Mountains as you approach them from the North. Author's Collection.

communication. On the east side of the mountain, there was a secret entry to a cavern where the Sata Exiponi or Dog Soldier organization met in secret. The warriors who were members of this group used rawhide ladders so they could enter the secret chamber only from the top of the mesa. They met at definite intervals and discussed important decisions that needed to be made for the welfare of the tribe.

While the Comanches lived in this area, they saw a meteorite fall nearby. They called this fire rock a gift from the Sun, so they gave it a special place in the hidden cavern. Civil Chief Mope Chocope told a white man that the meteorite had been kept there for 100 years. According to Comanche history, in 1805 the cavern caved in and buried the fire rock under many tons of sand. But this isn't the end of the fire rock story.

Many years later some industrious Comanche women uncovered the rock, and the tribe called Antelope Eaters planned to move the rock to another training camp on the Red River. With much tugging and effort, the heavy rock was loaded onto poles so it could be dragged. This project continued for two years as they worked on it when they could. Finally Indian Agent Robert S. Neighbors wrote a letter about the fire rock in 1856. He said at that time he took the rock to San Antonio. The famous rock had one more trip because in 1859, it was taken to Austin to be exhibited in the Texas Memorial Museum. The Santa Anna area had one more interesting discovery related to Indians. According to a website article by the Santa Anna Chamber of Commerce, a boulder with the head of an Indian carved into it was located on one of the peaks several decades ago. T.T. Perry was believed to have carved this profile in the 1800s. Perry placed the words, "Santa Anna" below the carving made on a two ton boulder.

At that time, he also carved the outline of an Eagle on another boulder. The Santa Anna Sand Plant, which was operating on Santa Anna Peaks, shut down in the 1960s. Their equipment was sold to a company in Arkansas. The owner took the two ton boulder with him to Guion, Arkansas. He tried to blast out the Eagle profile from the other rock, but that rock flew into many pieces. In 1996 citizens from Santa Anna made an agreement with the sand plant in Arkansas to retrieve the large stone from their state. They brought it home, and it now resides at the base of Santa Anna peaks.

Not all the Comanche tribes were working peacefully with each other as the ones at Santa Anna Peak were. About 1858, there were many hostile Comanche living outside of Texas while a fairly large group of Comanche were living on the Brazos Indian Reserve. The feelings between these two groups were not good. Indians always had ways to carry messages, and Chief Buffalo Hump, a Penateka who sided with the northern Comanche, delivered a severe one. He told the friendly Indians at the Clear Fork Brazos Reservation that he was coming down to wipe them out. When he finished with them, he intended to get the soldiers at Fort Chadbourne, which was north of present day Bronte, Texas.

According to Dr. Mildred P. Mayhall in "The Battle of Wichita Village" in the *True West Magazine* of February, 1972, Captain (Brevet Major) Earl Van Horn was ordered by General Twiggs to go northward and chastise those Comanche who were stirring up trouble in the Oklahoma Territory. As Twiggs was planning this invasion of the Comanche, officers at nearby Fort Arbuckle were planning with the Department of the Interior to seek treaties with these same Oklahoma tribes. Even so, Van Horn went along with his plans to invade the northern Comanche, but he wanted a little help from the friendly Indians.

He let it be known that he thought the Texas Rangers and the volunteers had been given the help of the friendly Indians while he had to go it alone in past conquests. He was criticizing Indian Agent Shapley P. Ross. After Ross denied this statement, he convinced Van Dorn to use the friendly Tonkawa Indians in his march toward Oklahoma. About one hundred-thirty-five guides and warriors were rounded up to go on the trip. They included leaders Shot-in-the-Foot of the Waco tribe and Tawakoni Jim of the Tawakonis. Tankawas, Ionis, and Anadahcos were included. But the soldiers wouldn't let any Comanche go because they might have relatives in the Oklahoma Territory. They didn't want to pit Comanche against Comanche.

Agent Ross, with his son Sul Ross accompanied the friendly Indians who went with Van Dorn and his men. Delaware scout, Jim Shaw, also helped Agent Ross on this trip. Four companies of the Second Cavalry left September 15, 1858 and headed north. They crossed the Red River and eventually camped in the Wichita Mountains. While Van Dorn sent out scouts to find the Comanche camp, some of his friendly Indians also found the camp and warned the Comanche about the soldiers camped nearby. Van Dorn planned to attack the Indian camp, but the soldiers had a much longer ride to find them than they had first planned.

After riding for 32 hours without much rest, Van Dorn's scouts found the Comanche village. The Tonkawa scouts managed to drive off the Comanche's herd of horses, so when the soldiers opened fire, the Indians were caught off-guard. Some ran for their horses only to find they were gone. Their women and children ran for the brush nearby so they could hide. Since the Indians were caught in their village, the fighting soon became hand-to-hand combat. The village was pretty well surrounded with the four companies of soldiers. Several soldiers went after a group of fleeing Comanche, but stopped when they realized they were women and children. Ross did see a white child in the group. Just as Lt. Cornelius Van Camp and C.C. Alexander charged to grab the child, Indians struck them down with arrows. Ross' gun misfired, and he was shot with an arrow also. He would have died at the hands of an approaching Indian if it hadn't been for Lt. James Harrison coming to his rescue and killing the Indian.

Finally the shots fired less frequently and the surviving Indians ran away. When the battle was over, the men discovered that Van Dorn had been shot with an arrow in his abdomen and one in his wrist. Soldiers went to Fort Arbuckle and brought an ambulance so they could load the wounded. After Van Dorn felt well enough to be moved, he returned to Mississippi for an extended time to recuperate. There would be more battles in the future, but not with Van Dorn.

White settlers living near the Oklahoma border met the Comanche much later than the settlers of Central Texas as was the case of Kate and Ephraim Polly. According to the *Lipscomb County History* published in 1976, this couple lived in a dugout on Morgan Creek in 1874. One morning Ephraim left the dugout to tend to a sick buffalo hunter. He had been a hospital steward in the Army, so he was often called to help out a neighbor. Kate was left alone with their two children, two-year-old Katie and four-year-old Annie.

After Ephraim had been gone awhile, Kate looked outside the dugout. She saw hundreds of horseback Indians carrying bows or rifles. They encircled her cabin and the spokesperson came inside. With gestures and painful pinches, he indicated his men wanted food. "Food for hundreds of men," surely Kate wondered how she could do that.

She finally decided to cook them pancakes, so she lit the fire, put her apron on, and mixed the batter. As she cooked the pancakes, the Indians filed into her home and grabbed several hot pancakes a piece. She decided they didn't need butter or syrup because they ate them so quickly. She would get one batch cooked, and more would come. If she didn't cook fast enough to suit them, the Indians would pinch her again. Kate cooked all day, and finally at sundown, she had used up all her flour that was in the 192 pound flour barrel.

At this point Kate was exhausted, but not everyone had received food. Kate decided she didn't care anymore. She grabbed her two-year-old, went outside, and while setting on a log, she let her youngest nurse. After awhile, some Indians motioned to her that they wanted more food, and they pinched her. She was so tired that she didn't care anymore. Kate lifted her finger and pulled it across her neck as she gave the sign of killing her. She had one nice thought. She wouldn't have to wash anymore dishes if they killed her.

The Indians must have admired her stamina because they left her alone, mounted their horses, rounded up Polly's' milk cows and left. This same party of Indians showed up at Adobe Walls in Hutchinson County at dawn June 27, 1874. They greatly outnumbered the buffalo hunters at that community, but Billy Dixon was a good shot. He killed the Indian's medicine man. When the medicine man toppled from his horse, the Indians took it as a bad omen. Only two defenders died in this incident, but it was the beginning of the Red River War.

When Ephraim returned to his dugout, he saw so many unshod horse tracks around his dugout that he was shocked that his family was O.K. By his estimate, there could have been 700 horses at his dugout that day. The Pollys thought that losing their milk cows was a small loss considering what could have happened. They were a bit surprised when a short time later, they saw their milk cows coming down the trail to their house. But the experience was scary enough that the Pollys moved back to Fort Hays in Kansas. They didn't return to Hemphill County until 1885. Ephraim was later elected their first county judge. They lived out the rest of their lived at that home.

Santa Anna Indian Stone outline of a warrior found near the Santa Anna Mountains

Chief Yellow Wolf painted by Capt. Arthur T. Lee. Courtesy of West Texas Collection, Angelo State University.

Chapter 9 Tankersley and the Kickapoo

Descendants of Richard Franklin Tankersley, early West Texas cattleman, related that Richard said, "I told the Indians that I'd leave their buffalo alone if they'd leave my cattle alone." Richard Tankersley and his family lived as isolated ranchers in the 1860s, far from any settlers. But they had several different tribes as their Texas neighbors and survived to tell about it. The young couple came from Mississippi to Texas a short time after his marriage to Annie Eleanor, (Ellen) Allen in 1848 in Jackson, Mississippi. After overcoming malaria while living near the Louisiana border, Richard pushed westward until he and Annie stopped in San Saba County with their young family.

In that area of low rolling hills, they lived near what the children called The Springs. As a child, his daughter Elizabeth leaned over to look closely at the bubbling springs. In her memories written many years later, she told of seeing bright colored Indian beads lying on the river bottom at the springs, also called Richland Springs. For this reason, they knew their cabin was situated on an old Indian campground Richard's Dad, George Tankersley, came westward a few years later with his wife and met his son at the river camp. George was registered as a voter in San Saba County in 1857. On January 25, 1857, George was on the first list of jurors from which a grand jury was selected for that county.

After living at the Springs for two years, Richard decided to head toward Coleman County. When he left this home, the John Duncans moved into the two cabins the Tankersley families left vacant near the Springs. Indians came back to the area after the Tankersleys departed, so they made life hard for any white settler who thought about living there. Eventually several families lived at the Springs and for protection from the Indians, they built a little fort. They called it Fort Duncan.

While Richard and Annie lived in Coleman County, the Indian attacks escalated in Texas. As more Texans were killed by the Indians, pleas for protection were directed towards the

Federal government. Finally the cries for help were answered with forts. The only problem was the location of these fortresses. Some were built along the northern boundary, the Red River; and others were clustered along the southern boundary, the Rio Grande. But Richard and Annie lived in Central Texas, far from any protection. The Indians who attacked settlers in Coleman County were on horseback and usually fired at their prey using bows and arrows.

Some Indian chiefs tried to keep the treaties and work with the white men. Old Owl was a Comanche Chief who attempted to get along with his neighbors and keep the peace treaties. He was a majestic looking specimen as he rode his horse with no shirt. His bronze body was decorated with shiny armbands and headdress flowing almost to the ground. He often draped a buffalo robe about his hips. Old Owl's presence demanded respect because of his leadership.

This great leader died in 1849, and the Indian policy toward settlers changed. Buffalo Hump was the next in command, and he shared little interest in Old Owl's treaties. He often led a raiding party whenever the mood struck him. Later in the 1850s, his tribe was mostly in Oklahoma, but Buffalo Hump still encouraged his young braves to raid along the Colorado and San Saba Rivers.

After hearing many such stories of Indian raids, Texas Governor Hardin R. Runnels received authority from the Texas Legislature to put troops across the interior frontier areas. With $70,000 appropriated, he commissioned John Williams to "enroll a company of twenty mounted men from Llano and San Saba counties for protection against the Indians." This information was recorded by Marvin Schultz in "Richard Franklin Tankersley: The Patriarch of West Texas," *Fort Concho South Plains Journal Summer 1991*. Richard joined the group of Texas Rangers May 24, 1858, but in their first 60 days in the field, they didn't fight any Indians.

Many of the troopers served awhile, returned home to take care of their crops and livestock, and came back to the Rangers when needed. Richard re-enlisted in the fall of 1858.

They were told to scout one-fourth of the time and not be away from

Richard F. Tankersley, early rancher in Three Rivers area. Courtesy of Fort Concho National Historic Landmark

home more than two months at a time unless they were fighting Indians. These Rangers watched the calendar to pinpoint the full of the moon. Indian raids always increased when the moon light aided their foray.

The Ranger schedule also varied according to a soldier's crops. The men tried to be home when it was time to plant their fields. Also they had to make their own living and pay for their horses, saddles, and bridles that they used as soldiers. Every ranger also needed a good rifle or a double-barreled shotgun, a pistol, and plenty ammunition. A mercantile store in Austin did provide rations for the Rangers the two months they were away from home.

When Richard re-enlisted, he was with a group of soldiers who were supposed to protect an area from Brown County to the old Mission Santa Cruz de San Saba, downstream from present day Menard on the San Saba River. From Richard's home in Coleman County, he would have to ride about 75 miles to reach Menard. They covered a wide area, and John Williams led Company G, Frontier Regiment of the Texas Rangers on this trip.

Richard and the other Rangers rode many miles through barren, rolling hills with few trees and no settlers. The prairie grass was so thick near the rivers that the soldiers had to cut through the grass to water their horses. On the prairies they passed through, they often saw miles of freshly burned land. The Rangers knew the Indians did the burning, but they wondered why. The soldiers finally discovered that in the spring these burned areas had fresh green grass, so they realized the Indians were planning for their horses to have plenty forage. The Indians also used the burns to drive away enemies such as other tribes or the soldiers when they got too close to the Indian's camp.

Most likely Richard saw the South Concho River, which was about 40 miles from the San Saba on this trip. It is likely he saw this beautiful place because in 1864, Richard moved his family to the springs on the South Concho River, about 25 miles south of the future town of Saint Angela, San Angelo.

On the 1860 Census of Brown County, Richard's family was included because Coleman County was a part of Brown County at that time. Richard and his wife Annie were listed as thirty-one years old. They had the following children: Elizabeth, eight; Clara, five; and George Washington, three. Baby Fayette was born sometime during this year but wasn't on the census. Their slaves, Betty and George were still with the family.

Other entrees on the 1860 Brown County Census of the same area made for some interesting deductions. One George Tankersley, who was also thirty-one was listed as a farmer who was born in Georgia. A ten year old Marcus D. L. Tankersley was on the roll but never mentioned as their child. Richard had a sister, Sarah, living with them, and their neighbor T. J. Priddy was a twenty-five year old stock raiser from Alabama. He was very interested in Richard's sister, Sarah.

In 1856 a fort was built on Mukewater Creek in southern Coleman County. This fort was made of picket walls, so it wasn't very fancy. Upright logs were placed close together in a trench and the cracks between the poles were filled with mud. Usually a tarp or thatch roof completed the building. Seven soldiers came down with malaria at this fort and the water supply was very inadequate. The government finally decided to move Camp Colorado north about 20 miles to the Jim Ned Creek.

When the soldiers moved out, somebody moved in. Richard Tankersley was ready to move his cattle to graze near the vacant fort. Richard thought the picket structure was O.K. for his brood, so Annie lived in some pretty interesting places. A few miles east of the fort the Tankersleys had neighbors, Moses and Lydia Jackson and their seven children. In October of 1858, the Jackson family decided to have an outing on the Pecan Bayou with their neighbors, the Kings and the Kirkpatricks. The plan was for the men to cut down pecan trees for board timber while the rest of the families picked pecans. But before the Jacksons ever got to the meeting place, a band of Indians attacked their family. Moses and his wife, Lydia, were killed instantly along with the children, Louise and I.E.

The Indians grabbed two other children, Joshua and Rebecca, as captives and sped away. The soldiers at Camp Colorado were told of the massacre and soon followed the Indians. Richard and his neighbor T.J. Priddy followed the Indian trail into Coryell County and back through Comanche County along with the troops. A group of Coryell County citizens also helped in the chase. This episode lasted for thirteen days. When the Indians realized the troopers were gaining on them, they pushed the two children off their horses and sped away.

The distraught children hid in the bushes. Eventually, the soldiers marching along the road heard the crying children in the bushes and rescued them. The troopers wrapped the scared and scratched children in a soldier's overcoat while they rode to the Tankersley's home. Since the day was bitter cold, the soldiers decided to quit their chase after they found the boy and girl.

In the warmth of the Tankersley house, the children explained why they were scratched so much. The Indians made them ride a pony with no reins to control the horse. The horse ran wherever he wanted and scraped the bushes. The Jackson children stayed with the Tankersleys until their relatives came for them.

Two people in the Tankersley household who were really frightened over the Indian attack were Annie's slaves, Betty and George. They had endured a lot on this trip from Mississippi but they were very scared of the Indians. Annie told Betty and George that they could go home, and they did.

When the Civil War broke out, all the troops left forts like Camp Colorado, so the Texas Rangers were activated again. Richard re-enlisted and had commanding officer Col. James M. Norris. It wasn't very long before the Rangers realized they were fighting a losing battle. A few men were scattered over too great a distance, and they had little ammunition. As if these challenges were not enough, the men came down with the measles. Richard was fortunate not to have the measles, which might have been due to the fact that he had four children at home. Maybe he had already been exposed.

Morale of the troops broke down and Lt. W. J. Perryman was court-martialed for playing cards. Surely there were more problems with his behavior than playing cards. Other officers were removed for disciplinary action, so there seemed to be no desire by the men to serve in the home militia, also called the Texas Rangers. By January of 1862, Richard decided to leave the Texas Rangers. Huge herds of buffalo congregated at the springs where the Tankersleys lived. The herd was so large that they clogged the springs up with mud and silt so much that the springs couldn't run. This was in the winter of 1863. When the big animals left, Richard dug with a shovel in an attempt to unclog the springs. After days of working in the mud that had been trampled, he began to see the water oozing from the cleaned areas.

Richard had learned a lot about working with cattle from his neighbor John Chisholm, who had his headquarters on Mukewater Creek. John and Richard only worked their cattle when it was time to brand or start a trail drive. Several times they lost cattle to the Indian raids in their area. Richard and John found out in a round about way that their cattle were stolen. The Indians who stole the cattle, sold the cattle to indifferent Indian agents. Indians got a bonus two ways in this case. The warriors who stole the cattle got money for them. Their Indian friends who were on the reservations also received some good meat to eat.

When the two ranchers, Richard and John Chisholm, met to sort out their cattle, Chisholm mentioned his cattle grazing all the way to the Concho Rivers. Three streams carried names: South Concho, Main Concho, and Middle Concho. Richard had seen that area when he rode on a scouting trip with the Rangers several years before. He liked what he saw on the scouting trip, so he began to formulate a plan to move his operation to the land of the Conchos.

By the spring of 1864, Richard Tankersley moved to the head of the South Concho River. His slaves had returned to their home in Mississippi, and Richard had buried both his mother and father in Texas. Now the Tankersley clan included Richard, Annie, and the children. Annie had five or six children when they moved. Henry Martin was born sometime during 1864. The other children included Elizabeth, Clarissa, George Washington, Fayette, and Mary. The oldest child, Elizabeth was 12 that year, and George Washington was seven, so Richard didn't have much family help moving his livestock.

When their ox-drawn wagon rolled southwestward, Richard had seven hundred longhorn cattle and forty-five horses to drive. It is unknown whether any of his neighbors helped him on the drive, but people like T. J. Priddy may have helped if Sarah, his girl friend, made the move to the new home. Annie must have been exhausted after riding the wagon all day, but she had to cook supper for the family using only an open campfire. They reached the South Concho River after traveling for many days.

Annie Tankersley lived from 1828 to 1902 and took care of a large family in a home far from civilization. Courtesy of Fort Concho Historical Landmark.

Years later the Tankersley's son, Fayette, described the place they called home in a newspaper article in *The Mertzon Star.* He said the country was a beautiful site with wild flowers blooming and grass that was stirrup high. He said the sparkling river had many fish. Thick woods and dense undergrowth protected the wildlife. They saw huge flocks of turkeys, antelope, and deer roaming in herds of thousands. Fayette saw wild mustangs, coyotes, and panthers. The streams were alive with fish, and beavers built their dams in all the rivers. The first fall they lived on the South Concho, the buffalo came in herds that "in the distance they looked like great swarms of flies." In the spring time of the year, the buffalo left the South

Concho to head northwest, but in the winter they returned. Fayette said that lonely, howling lobos followed the buffalo.

When Richard and Annie arrived at the springs on the South Concho, there was no house or any kind of protection built for their family. For many weeks, Annie cooked all their meals over a campfire and washed their dirty clothes the same way. The smallest children and Annie probably slept in their wagon until Richard could make a cabin.

One day in early January of 1865, Richard saw several Indians walking up the road in broad daylight. He grabbed his gun and prepared to die protecting his family. As the Indians got closer, one Indian said, "Me no fight. Me friend." They gave the sign of peace and Richard relaxed a bit. They were Kickapoo who had come from Oklahoma and were on their way to old Mexico. They drew marks in the dirt so that Richard understood they were looking for lost horses. Richard sketched in the dirt the brand on some of his lost horses also.

After Annie got over her initial fright, she invited the Indians into her home. Daughter Elizabeth later related that the Indians looked over the house carefully as they went from room to room. She said they opened the drawers and lifted lids but didn't bother anything. Annie, being the gracious Southern host, gave them honey that was still in the honeycomb. They scooped it up in their hands and ate it. Mary, being one of the younger children, was scared and hid behind the door. One squaw tried to give her some beads through a narrow space between the door and the wall.

After the cordial visit, the Indians left the Tankersleys, and the next morning Richard was surprised to see his missing horse in his corral. Who were these friendly Indians?

The Kickapoo called the Great Lakes region of America their home in the 1600s. At that time, they spent the summer months growing food crops and having religious ceremonies, but they hunted during the cool months. The Kickapoo moved about on the prairies killing their winter meat and collecting edible wild plants. But when other tribes as well as the pushy white men caused problems for the Kickapoo, they headed west. History verifies that some of the Kickapoo people couldn't get along with each other, so they broke into three distinct groups. Some bands of Kickapoo stayed in Kansas and Oklahoma while others turned their horses toward Texas and Mexico. This latter group of Indians were among the ones that Tankersley met. Throughout their history, these Kickapoo were mentioned as the ones who had kept their traditions and lived isolated from other tribes. They didn't want to fight other groups unless it was necessary.

Strange as it may seem, the Kickapoo were invited to settle in Texas by representatives of the Spanish government. These Spanish soldiers who were present in Texas thought these Indians might act as a buffer against the increasing number of Americans who wanted to settle in Texas. What the leaders south of the Rio Grande didn't anticipate was the war that took place in Texas. In 1836, the Texas Revolution brought about a new republic with its own government. Kickapoo leaders adjusted to this predicament by joining the displaced Cherokees in Texas. Chief Bowles of the Cherokee made an agreement with the Kickapoo so the two tribes could aid each other.

As the frontier became more crowded, the Kickapoo alliance with Cherokee and Delaware warriors began to assault settlers along the Rio Grande. One time this combination of Kickapoo and Cherokee attacked a group of surveyors who looked up from their instruments to see 300 Indians riding toward them. Twenty-five surveyors were killed. Deeds like this increased until Texas President, Mirabeau B. Lamar decided to force all the Indians out of Texas. Many of the Kickapoo crossed the Rio Grande into Mexico and worked for the Mexican government. For many of this tribe, such a move was alright because the Kickapoo had already made Mexico their home and helped the Mexican government so much that they were awarded 78,000 acres of land near Zaragoza and Remolino. In 1852 the tribe traded this grant for 17,352 acres at El Nacimiento and an equal amount in Durango, which they never used.

The Kickapoo who Richard Tankersley met, were planning to join this band who were so thoroughly entrenched in Mexico. Few Indians wanted to take the Union or the Confederate side

Kickapoo wickiup shown in 1880s. Courtesy of the U.S. National Archives

of the Civil War, so the Kickapoo were staying neutral by making their home in Mexico. But a few days later after talking with the Tankersley family, those same Indians were attacked by 500 Texas Rangers and Confederate soldiers in what was called the Battle of Dove Creek. The hostilities took place January 8, 1865, about 12 miles northwest of Richard's home. Now the Kickapoo were engaged in a battle involving some Confederate troops.

Later Richard and Annie found out that about 2,000 Kickapoo were camped on Dove Creek. They had so many teepees that their camp was about a mile long. The soldiers had followed the Indians' trail from the Clear Fork on the

Brazos in north Texas, but they hadn't bothered to find out if the Indians were friendly or not.

When the soldiers fired on the Kickapoo, the Indians found shelter in the hills near the river and drove the soldiers back. Some of the Kickapoo such as a young woman named Oo-lath-la-hi-na thought the soldiers were confusing them with another tribe of warring Indians. She could read and write, so she thought she could reason with the troopers. Oo-lath-la-hi-na stepped in front of her tribe so the soldiers could see her. While holding her white flag, she said, "I'll go out and talk with the white Captain. He thinks we are Comanches. The white men won't shoot a woman with a flag." But Oo-lath-la-hi-na was wrong. She was killed with a white man's bullet.

The battle continued all day, but thirty-six troopers lost their lives, many more than the Indians lost. As soon as the battle was over, the Kickapoo left the encampment heading south. They were in such haste that they left cooking pots and many buffalo robes.

The reason the Kickapoo headed straight for the Rio Grande was because they knew some Kickapoo had lived successfully in that area for many years. As early as June of 1839, a band of Kickapoo, along with Cherokee, Delaware, and Caddo warriors entered the Mexican town of Matamoros. This group included about 80 warriors who had traveled a great distance on their trip from east Texas. As the years went by, the Mexican military used these warriors to prevent attacks from other militant Indian tribes by mustering the Indian braves into the Mexican military. A formal agreement was made between the Indians and the Mexican government on June 27, 1850 when Wild Cat, a Seminole chief acted as the spokesman for the Indian tribes. He led the Kickapoo and the Seminole warriors when he signed an agreement between the Inspector General of the Eastern Military Colonies, Atoio Maria Juaregui, and the Indians. Under this agreement, the Indians received 70,000 acres of land. Also they would obey the laws of the land, maintain good relations with the United States, and provide warriors when necessary to curb the influx of Comanches and other barbarous tribes. One of the most important factors in this treaty was the fact that the Kickapoo didn't have to change their lifestyle. Their unique customs and habits could be continued without any problems and this meant a lot to them.

As the years went by, some Kickapoo decided to move back into the United States and live near the border town of Eagle Pass. About 500 Kickapoo made this trip, so the only ones left in Mexico were nine men, seven women and four children. They were moved deeper into Mexico because the Mexican government feared that slave traders would capture them.

When the Civil War erupted, both the north and the south tried to persuade the Kickapoo to fight for them, but they refused both offers. In 1866 Benito Juarez located the tribe near Masques where they were given land.

But back in January of 1865, the Kickapoo left their camp on Dove Creek in great haste. The next day Richard rode to the battle site. He was very angry at the soldiers for firing on friendly Indians, but he did help bury the dead. One man he buried was a soldier Richard had ridden with when they were Texas Rangers. A day or two later, the remaining soldiers were headed home in snow and freezing rain. Richard told them how to get to John Chisholm's Ranch in Coleman County, which was about 70 miles away. One injured soldier died on the way and another died at Chisholm's ranch. It was January 17 that the weary troops made it to safety and got about 1,500 pounds of flour. The men got enough provisions at Chisholm's ranch store that they were able to ride to Camp Colorado.

When this band of Kickapoo made it to the Mexican border, they joined other members of their tribe and attacked the white settlers along the border with the help of Mexican guerrillas. These men were led by Vicente Cordova. This combination of Indians and Mexicans wrecked havoc along the Rio Grande. Texas' President, Mirabeau B. Lamar, hated Indians anyway, so he began a crusade to remove all Indians from Texas.

The Battle of Dove Creek should never have happened. It turned the friendly Kickapoo into a warring tribe. As soon as they made it across the Rio Grande, they often had raiding parties that terrified ranchers on the U.S. side of the river.

Richard never heard from them again, but the Comanche and Kiowa raided periodically in his area. When Richard went to San Antonio to get supplies or if he drove his steers to market, he left Annie alone with the children. Many a night, Annie set up with a gun in her hands, and she said she heard the Indians walking outside of her house. The next morning they saw moccasin tracks in the dirt and usually one or more horses were missing from the corral.

The Tankersley children related years later that, "We don't know why the Indians didn't kills us." The only thing the kids could figure out was that the Indians knew their mother and father were very brave. Several instances verify that idea.

One time Richard was trying to pen his dairy cows. They always had milk cows for the family's supply of milk and butter. When he tried to round them up this particular time, a buffalo calf was in the herd. Richard roped the calf and tied it to a tree so it was easier to get the cows penned. Later he returned to untie the buffalo calf. He found it shot through with arrows. The Indians had watched them pen their cows. It seemed like the warriors were saying, "We watched you and saw it all."

Even picking berries could be a dangerous past time. One day Mary and some of the other children were picking the tasty fruit when some Comanche Indians came by. The children hid immediately in the brush. They were so scared that they stayed in their hiding place for two days. Some Texas Rangers finally found them and took them home to some very distraught parents.

They would have stolen his two mules, but they could not drive them. The mules kept turning back toward the Tankersley house, so the Indians gave up trying to maneuver them along the trail.

Although the Indians didn't harm the Tankersleys, they loved to steal their horses. One time while the family was on the South Concho, the Indians stole all the horses Richard had. They would have stolen his two mules, but they couldn't drive them. The mules kept turning back toward the Tankersley house, so the Indians gave up trying to steal them. Richard caught up with one mule and saddled him. But when he tried to pursue the Indians, he couldn't make the stubborn creature go. On the next trip to San Antonio, Richard got provisions and horses, but he sold the mules.

One of Richard F. Tankersley's houses that was 6 miles east of present-day San Angelo. House is still standing. Photo by Francis Hill.

While ranching in such an isolated area, Richard worked his livestock himself and put in long hours. His young sons rode for long stretches also. Fayette remembered being in the saddle for thirty-six hours at one stretch. He was a husky boy of nine when they left the South Concho in 1868, so he started working cattle at a very young age. He related that his Dad put in many eighteen-hour days astride his horse.

By 1866 the Indians stepped up their hostilities in the area where the Tankersleys lived. Richard had a visit from Buck Neighbors who lived downstream from him about three miles. Later the settlers in the area planned to meet at the Ben Ficklin Stage headquarters downstream about 20 miles from Richard's house. At the meeting, the settlers decided they needed to go to Fort Mason and ask for help. The settlers felt the Indian attacks were to numerous for the settlers to survive. Buck Neighbors said he would make the 100 miles trip if Richard would loan him his fast horse.

Surprisingly rider and horse made it to Fort Mason, and within the same year, soldiers visited the Concho River area to select a site for a fort. They chose a place near Ben Ficklin's Stage Headquarters and began the fort as a tent city. As the years went by, Fort Concho had permanent buildings and the troops began to control the Indian population.

Richard Tankersley continued to own more cattle, so they were spread out from the Colorado River on the north to back southward to the Spring Creek and Concho River area. The Indians didn't quit harassing the ranchers though. Ranchers like Richard near Saint Angela, and R.S. Coggin and John R. Parks near Brownwood had lost a lot of cattle to the Indians in the 1870s. Some of these ranchers brought depredation suits against the government for their loss of cattle and horses soon after it happened. But Richard never got around to suing until he did so in 1892.

The case was number 6501 of Richard F. Tankersley vs. the United States and the Kiowas and Comanche Indians. He stated his loss in 1870 happened in Tom Green County. He asked for $94,618   for the loss of 5,100 cattle and many horses. Richard filed this petition January 13, 1892 through his attorney, Silas Hare. The attorney had problems getting the details because the event happened in 1970 and they were suing in 1892, some twenty-two years later.

Richard did have plenty of witnesses called on his behalf. His children G.W. Tankersley, Fayette Tankersley, Elizabeth Emerick, and Clarissa Frary testified in their father's behalf. He also had rancher friends who tried to help his case. Men who substantiated his story were R.S. Coggin, B.F. Jenkins, N.T. Guest, W.N. Adams, John R. Parks, John F. Hart, J.L. Lawson, G.B. Mann and James Dofflemyer.

Richard began his testimony by explaining that he was born in the State of Mississippi and came to Texas in 1852. He listed the places he had lived as Williamson County for four years, San Saba County two years, Brown County for six years, which included Coleman County, and then he said he moved to Tom Green in 1864.

Richard said the cattle thievery began when he ranched eight miles west of San Angelo in 1870 or 1872. At that time he said he had over seven thousand cattle and the larger part of them were beef steers, threes and older. He said his cattle ranged over the head draws of Spring Creek and the Conchos. He testified that John Chisholm, his old friend from near Coleman, had livestock in this area as well as John Parks.

Richard described how one of his men saw sign of the Indian trail on which the cattle were driven. When he was told about the incident, Tankersley then notified General Hatch at Fort Concho, and a party was organized to follow the Indian trail. The group included a squad of soldiers under Lieut. Shoemaker, ranchers John Drennan, Bob Miller, Ben Jenkins, and Richard. They followed the Indians' path about 125 miles to the head of the Colorado River. After following the trail about thirty miles the second day out, the group struck another set of tracks, a large path about fifteen miles from where they were. The big trail was a half mile wide and about two weeks old as Tankersley described it. He knew that because of the decomposed bodies of cattle he saw.

Richard testified that he found a good many dead cattle on the Indian path. He could trail them by the buzzards that were flying about the dead carcasses. He saw some dead cattle with arrows in them, but he thought most of the herd had been run to death, since it was so hot in July. He explained that the cattle were probably dead two weeks and the brands showed some belonged to R.S. Coggin, John Parks, John Chisholm, and some were his. He said the trail was littered with Indian saddles, moccasins, and trinkets.

Richard also described seeing the remains of an Indian camp along the worn path. He said the camp might have been there for a week. Teepees made of brush and grasses were still standing in an area where they camped. Then he explained how they actually saw some Indians with cattle near the head draws of the Colorado River:

"I saw six Indians, and Liet. Shoemaker ordered us to charge and four of us run them about five miles, but did not overtake them. We captured about 100 head of cattle from the Indians, which belonged to Cog gins and Parks and others, and I met some of my cattle coming back on the trail. This large trail of cattle I saw had come right out of our range and judging from the trail, I should think there was at least ten thousand cattle driven over it."

Richard Tankersley was definite when he said he had about 7,500 head of cattle before the raid, but he explained his herd was reduced to about 300 cattle he could find afterwards. Stripped of practically all of his cattle, Tankersley took the remaining few and penned them every night in San Angelo. He said he did this in fear he would lose the rest of them on a raid.

When he testified about the loss of horses, the dates were not clear, so the petition was changed to ask for the loss of 5,100 head of cattle at a price of $10 a head, or $51,000. R.S. Coggin testified in behalf of Tankersley and substantiated his story. He explained that he had cattle on the same range and lost them at the same time as Richard did. Coggin restated that John Parks and himself had lost cattle in the same raid and had received a judgment from the government.

The defendant had only one witness, a clerk of the court of Tom Green County, Ed Duggan. He explained that Richard testified that he owned an irrigated farm in Tom Green County in 1871 when in reality he did not buy the property there until 1873. Even Tankersley's own sons, Fayette and G.W. agreed on the 1873 date, but this discrepancy did not affect the final outcome of the trail. In the final decision of the court, R.F. Tankersley was given only $23,000. This claim was finally recorded in 1902.

By this time, Richard and his children had cattle spread over many counties. He continued riding his horses to help round-up and brand the cattle until he came down with pneumonia in December of 1912. A few days later, he died at the age of 84. He was buried in a fenced cemetery west of the big house he owned in Tankersley, Texas, a small community between Mertzon and San Angelo.

By 1870, many tribes including the Kickapoo were raiding all over Texas and especially along the Rio Grande border. The Texas government called for military aid to stop the bloodshed. On May 18, 1873, Col. Ranald Mackenzie's Fourth United States Cavalry set about to squelch the Indian violence. Mackenzie had word that the Kickapoo would be on one of their major hunts at this time and would be away from their camp near Remolino. He attacked the camp with 400 soldiers and made quick work defeating the women, infirmed, aged, and children who were left in camp. Forty surviving Indians, mostly women and children, were captured, tied two or three to a horse, and marched to San Antonio.

Later this remnant of the tribe was taken to Fort Gibson in Indian Territory. These Kickapoo women were held hostage because the soldiers hoped the fugitive warriors would surrender. About 317 Indians surrendered to the military and were taken to the Indian Territory where the rest of their family were waiting as captives. But many of the warriors refused to leave the area they called home. They regrouped at El Nacimiento along the Rio Grande.

To this day, there are Tankersley descendents scattered over Texas, and there are likewise Kickapoo Indians living along the Rio Grande River. At the present time, Kickapoo make their homes in Kansas, some in Oklahoma, and some in western Maverick County of Texas. The Texas Kickapoo live about 130 miles south of Eagle Pass in a 118 acre community called El Nacimiento. They had received this land in 1852 from the Spanish government, and their descendents managed to keep it. In a recent census, the Kickapoo along the Rio Grande number some 650 strong. Although they have remained true to their tribal culture and language, watching television has prompted more Kickapoo to learn the Spanish or English language than ever before.

During the summer months, it isn't unusual to see a large number of Kickapoo load up their gear and follow the migrant worker's trail. They pick fruit and vegetables in Texas as well as other western states. Since the Kickapoo live near the Texas-Mexico border, the United States has allowed them dual citizenship so they can work more easily on both sides of the border.

The Kickapoo did not own land in Texas until 1985. But because they have camped near the International Bridge between Pederas Negras, Coahuila, and Eagle Pass, Texas, they have long been identified with this state. An important law was passed on January 8, 1983, called Public Law 97-429. Under this law, the Kickapoo owned land near El Indio, Texas, and became known to the United States authorities as the Texas Band of the Oklahoma Kickapoos. This ruling made them eligible for federal aid, but they continue to call themselves the Mexican Kickapoo.

Some of the Kickapoo run the Lucky Eagle Casino in Eagle Pass. At the Lucky Eagle, visitors can enjoy the games or entertainment around the clock because the Casino is open 24-hour hours a day. Bingo as well as poker are very popular games to play by the visitors who frequent the casino. Recently the Casino has added the Rio Grande Buffet Restaurant and the Black Rocks Bar.

Various tribes are using different methods to make a living in present-day America and at the same time stay connected to their rich heritage.

Court of Claims.

(INDIAN DEPREDATION NO. 6501)

Richard F. Tankersley

v.

THE UNITED STATES and the *Kiowa and Comanche* INDIANS:

This case having been heard by the Court of Claims, the court, upon the evidence, makes the following

FINDINGS OF FACT.

I.

At the time of the depredations, hereinafter stated, the claimant *was a* citizen of the United States.

II.

On the year 1871, (alleged in the petition in the summer of 1870) in Tom Green county, State of Texas Indians belonging to the *Kiowa and Comanche tribes of Indians took and drove away* property of the kind and character described in the petition, the property of claimant , which was reasonably worth the sum of $*23,800.*

Said property was taken, as aforesaid, without just cause or provocation on the part of the owner or the agent in charge, and has never been returned or paid for.

A copy of the Depredation Claim given to the author by a Tankersley descendent, Loye Tankersley

A decorative Indian shield drawn by Sharon Gentry

Bibliography

Bibliography for Chapter 1
Books
Katz, William Loren, Black People Who Made the West.
Kelton, Elmer, The Indian in Frontier News, San Angelo, Talley Press, 1993.
Newcomb, W. W., Jr., The Indians of Texas, Austin, University of Texas Press, 1961.
Porter, Kenneth Wiggins, The Black Seminole: History of a Freedom seeking people: Univ. of Florida Press, 2013.
Smithwick, Noah, The Evolution of a State, Austin, University of Texas Press, 1983.
E-mail correspondence
With Russell Nowell, Curator of Old Guardhouse Museum, Fort Clark, Texas, June 24, 2013.
Internet Files
"Black   Seminole   Indian   Scouts   Assn.,"
http://seminolenation-indianterritory.org/blacksemindscouts.htm
"Black   Seminole   Scouts,"
http://tahaonline.org/handbook/online/articles/qlbgn
"Black   Seminole   Scouts,"
http://en.wikipedia.org/wiki/Black_Seminole_Scouts
"Bullis,   John   Lapham,"
http://www.tshaonline.org/handbook/onlinearticles/fbu19
"Fort   Duncan,"
http://www.tshaonline.org/handbook/online/articles/qbf17
"The Seminole-Negro Indian Scouts," by Karen Riles; http://www.texasindians.com/bsem.htm

Bibliography of Chapter2
Interviews

Interview with Larry Anderson, a Cherokee descendent, July 28, 2013, Sipe Springs, Texas.
Files
"A Brief History of the Cherokee" by Ira Kennedy
Books
An American Story of Defiant Chiefs, by Time Life Books, Virginia, 1997.
Jahoda, Gloria; The Trail of Tears, Wings Books, New York, 1975.
Newcomb, W.W., Jr; The Indians of Texas, University of Texas Press, 1961.
Magazines
A Biography of Duwali (Chief Bowles) 1756-1836 by Sibyl Creasey & Betty
Internet Files
Miller:http://www.overhillcherokee.com/bowles.htm.
Bean,   Peter   Ells; http://www.tshaonline.org/hndbook/online/articles/fbeo7
Chief   Duwali   Bowles   (http:www.findagrave.com/cgi-bin/fg.cgi?page=gr&Grid=837)
History of Texas Cherokees by D. L. Utsidihi Hicks, http://en.wiki/Principal_Chiefs_of_the_Cherokee
http://www.texascherokees.org/history1.html
Richard   Fields; http://www.tshaonline.org/handbook/online/articles/ffi05

The   1811-1812   Earthquakes;   http://en. Wikipedia.org/wiki/1811%E2%931812_New_Madtrid

Bibliography for Chapter 3
Books
Kelton, Elmer, The Indian in Frontier News, San Angelo, Talley Press, 1993.
Newcomb, W. W., Jr., The Indians of Texas, Austin, University of Texas Press, 1961.
Smithwick, Noah, The Evolution of a State, Austin, University of Texas Press, 1983.
Correspondence

A letter from Father Pinella to the Parent College of Quere'tar preserved in the Spanish Archives.

Magazines and Journals
Austermn,Wayne R., "Ambush and Siege at Paint Rock," Wild West, April 2010, Vol. 22
Chipman, Donald E., "In Search of cabeza de Vaca's Route Across Texas, Oct., 1987, Southwestern Historical Quarterly.

Museums
"Tonkawa as Texas Rangers," Texas Ranger Museum, Waco, Texas

Interviews
Phone call with Don Patterson, President of the Tonkawa, Tonkawa, Oklahoma, May 29, 2013

Internet Files
"Friends and Allies: The Tonkawa Indians and the Anglo-American,
http://digitalcommons.unl.edu/greatplainsquarterly/1904
"Jesse   Chisholm,"
http://www.rootsweb.ancestry.com/~okpcgc/people_and_famili es/fp101
"Placido,"
http://www.tshaonline.org/handbook/online/articles/
"Paint   Rock   Pictographs,"
http://www.texasbeyondhistory.net/plateaus/images/he4.html
"Presidio   La   Bahia,"
https://en.wikipedia.org/wiki/Presidio_La_BahC3%ADa
"The Official Website of The Tonkawa Tribe of Oklahoma,"
http://www.tonlawatribe.com/ceremonial.htm
"Tonkawa   Indians,"
http://www.tshaonline.org/handbook/online/articles/bmt68
"Tonkawa   Tribal   History,"
http://www.tonkawaribe.com/history.htm

Bibliography of Chapter 4
Articles
Ashmore, Tom. "Ancient Jumano Indians Meet 'The Lady in Blue."
Books

Fedewa, Marilyn H., Maria of Agreda: Mystical Lady in Blue. University of New Mexico Press: 2001

Hickerson, Nancy P., The Humanos: Hunters and Traders of the South Plains: Austin, University of Texas Press.

Newcomb, W. W., Jr., The Indians of Texas, Austin, University of Texas Press, 1961.

Wade, Maria F., Native Americans of the Texas Edwards Plateau, 1582 – 1799; Austin, University of Texas Press, 2003.

Internet Files

"Jumano   Indians," http://en.wikipedia.org/wik/Jumano_Indians

"Jumano   Indians," http://wwwtshaonline.orghandbook/online/articles/bmj07

Journals and Magazines

Fedewa, Marilyn H., "Jumano Native Americans Still revere Lady in Blue," Tradicion, Winter 2008.

Presentation

A speech by Eric Shroeder, "The Jumano Indians," given to the Concho Valley Archeological Society, September 26, 2013.

.

Bibliography of Chapter 5

Books

Editors of Time Life, The American Story: Defiant Chiefs. Alexandria. 1997.

Internet Files

"Kicking   Bird   (ca.1835-1875) http://www/tshaonline.org/handbook/online/article/fki03

"Kicking Bird) http://en.wikipedia.org/wiki/kicking_Bird

"Kiowa   Indians, http://www.tshaonline.org/handbook/online/articles/bmk10

Articles

Barton, Barbara, "Chief Lone Wolf," Ranch and Rural Living Magazine, April, 2012

Bibliography of Chapter 6

Books

Newcomb, W.W., Jr., The Indians of Texas, (Austin: University of Texas Press, 1961.

Internet Files

"Biographies of Great Lipan Chiefs," The Lipan Apache Tribe of Texas Official Website.

"Lipan   Apache   People," http://en.wikipedia.org/wiki/Lipan_Apache_People

Bibliography for Chapter 7

Articles

Ainsworth, Troy, "The Second Santa Fe Expedition: Jacob Snively and the Mission to Disrupt New Mexico Commerce in 1843," West Texas Historical Association Year Book, Vol. LXXXII, Oct., 2006.

Halley, Evetts J., "The Comanche Trade," Southwestern Historical Quarterly. Vol. 38, No. 3, Pp157 -176.

Books

Kelton, Elmer, The Indian in Frontier News, San Angelo, Talley Press, 1993.

Newcomb, W. W., Jr., The Indians of Texas, Austin, University of Texas Press, 1961.

Noah Smithwick, The Evolution of a State, Austin, University of Texas Press, 1983.

Internet Files

"Ciboleros," http://www.tshaonline.org/handbook/online/artidcles/poc02

"Comanchero Trails of the Texas High Plains." http://odomsinhappy.blogspot.com/

"Comancheros," http://plainshumanities.unl.edu/encyclopedia/doc/egp.ha.010

"The Comanchero Trade and Trails, by Jay W. Sharp" http://www.desertusa.com/mag04/nov/com.html

Reports

Whitefield, J. W., Overseer of Upper Arkansas Indian Agency; Report to the Secretary of State, "Report of the Commissioner of Indian Offices in 1854 and 1855.

Bibliography of Chapter 8

Books

"Kate and Ephraim Polly," Lipscomb County History Book 1976.

Linn, John J., Reminiscences of Fifty Years in Texas.

Roemer, Ferdinand, Texas, 185 to 1847. Originally written in 1849. Reprinted by Eakin Press, Austin, Texas.

Internet Files

"Ambush and Siege at Paint Rock", by Wayne R. Austerman.   http://www.historynet.com/ambush-andsiege-at-paint-rock.htm

"Comanche   Indian   Reservation," http://www.tshaonline.org/handbook/online/articles/bpc10

"Comanche   Timeline," http://www.comanchelanguage.org/Comanche%20Timeline.htm

"Conner-Family-Mekinges," http://www.connerprairie.org/Learn-And-Do/Indiana-History/Co

"Elm   Creek   Raid," http://www.tshaonline.org/handbook/online/articles/bte01

"Jesse   Chisholm," http://rootsweb.ancestry.com/~okpcgc/people_and_families/

"Linnville   Raid   of   1840," http://www.tshaonline.org/handbook/online/articlesbt101

"Meusebach,   John   O.," http://www.tshaonine.org/handbook/online/articles/fme33

"Jim   Shaw," http://www.tshaonline.org/handbook/online/articlesw/fsh11

"Roemer,   Ferdinand   von," http://www.tshaonline.org/handbook/online/articles/fro55

"Santa   Anna   Historical   Development Organization,"http://www.web-access.net/~hdo/features/extraordinary.html

Journals and Magazines

Campbell, Fred R., "Comanche Red Jackets," from diary of Capt. Don Francisco Amangual 1808, Bexar Archives, Univ. of Texas, Center of American History.

Cox, Mike, "Pancakes Saved the Day," Ranch & Rural Living Magazine, Aug. 2010.

Mayhall, Dr. Mildred P., "The Battle of Wichita Village," True West Magazine, Feb., 1972.

Parker, William, "Diary of 1854 Expedition through Unexplored Texas."

Richardson, Rupert N., "Jim Shaw, The Delaware," The Cyclone, Vol. XIX, Issue 2; Pp.3.
Newspaper Articles
"Gen. Tom Green," San Angelo Standard Times, June 1, 1889.
Thesis
Pelon, Linda, "Was Mountain named for Penatuhkah War Chief Santa Anna?

Bibliography Chapter 9
Interviews and Speeches
Interview with Dalton Tankersley of Hico, Texas, July 10, 1998. Dalton said his father was a cousin of
Richard F. Tankersley.
Jack Landers' speech on the "History of Native Plants in West Texas," Tom Green County Historical
Society, 1998.
Correspondence
Letter from Richard Peeples to Susan Miles, June 10, 1957.
Personal Papers from Clara Emerick Wheelberger to Hal M. Noelke, 1960-62.
Files
"Tankersley Files," West Texas Collection, Angelo State University. San Angelo, Texas
Books
Elmer Kelton, The Indian in Frontier News. (San Angelo: The Talley Press, 1993).
Grace Bitner, "R. F. Tankersley and Family, Pioneers of the Concho Country" West Texas Historical
Association Year Book 20 (October 1944).
T. R. Havins, Something About Brown. (Brownwood: Banner Printing, 1958).
Alma Ward Hamrick, The Call of the San Saba. (Austin: San Felipe Press. 1969.
Thomas Robert Havins, Camp Colorado: A Decade of Frontier Defense. (Brownwood: Brown Press,
1964.
J. Marvin Hunter, The Trail Drivers of Texas, (New York: Argosy-Antiquarian LTD, 1963).

Gloria Jahoda, The Trail of Tears, (New Jersey: Random House Publishing, 1975).

San Saba Historical Commission, "Richland Springs," San Saba County History 1856 – 1983.

Magazine and Newspaper Articles
Patricia Baker Eckert, "Yesteryears," San Angelo Standard Times 9 October 1980.

Candace Cooksey Fulton, "1858 Jackson Crossing Massacre," San Angelo Standard Times 17 May, 1998.

Marvin Schultz, "Richard Franklin Tankersley: The Patriarch of West Texas," Fort Concho South Plains

Journal, Summer 1991.

Index of Friendly Indians

A
Adams, W. N., 174
Adams-Onis Treaty, 53
Adelsverein Society for the Protection of Immigrants in Texas,143
Agreda, Mary, 80
Albuquerque, N.M.,
Alexander, C. C., 155
Alford, Agent Henry, 100
Allen, Eliza, 28
Amangual, Don Francisco, 136
American Indian Heritage Center of Texas, 38
Amp Johnson, 150
Anderson, Larry, 38
Anza, Juan Bautists de
Apache, 46, 48, 84
Apostal, Santiago, 125
Aquayo, Marquis de, 43, 44
Austin, Moses, 54
Austin, Stephen, 54
B
Bailey, David, 100
Battey, Thomas C., 92, 93
Battle of Dove Creek, 169 - 171
Battle of the Neches, 38
Bean, Peter Ellis, 27, 32
Bee, Hamilton P., 147
Ben Ficklin Stage Headquarters, 173
Bent, William, 94
BigTree (Chief), 96 - 98
Black Seminoles, 1 - 19
Bliss, Maj. Zenvas R., 9, 10
Bowles, Duwali, 21 – 40, 168
Bowles, John, 37
Boyce, James, 116
Brackettville, 15
Bradberry, John, 24
Brazos River, 43
Brooks, J.H., 18
Brown County, 162
Brown, Dan D., 139
Buffalo Hump (Chief), 138, 149 – 154, 160
Bullis, Lt. John Lapham, 1- -14
Burleson, Gen., 117
Butler, Gov. Pierce, 147, 148
Butler-Lewis Treaty of 1846, 143-144
C
Caddos, 170
Calhoun, John, 28
Camp Colorado, 163, 164
Camp Eagle Pass, 6
Canalizo, Valentin, 142
Carrasco, Gabriel, 86
Casa Blanca Creek, 140
Casa Grande Tribe, 76
Casatilla, Aloonso de, 71
Castro, Juan (Chief), 112 - 115
Ceballo, Juan Joseph, 45
Cherokee Tribe, 21 – 40, 170
Cherokees & Their Associated Band, 5, 26
Chief Iron Shirt, 12
Chief Johnson, 12, 13
Chief Poor Buffalo, 13
Chisolm, Bill, 55, 57
Chisolm, Jesse, 57, 58

Chisolm, John, 165,171,175
Cibolero, 131 - 134
Coggin, R.S., 174, 176
Coleman County, 159-162,175
Colley, Agent S.G., 95
Colley, Wiliam, 28
Colorado River, 43,174,175
Comancheros, 121- 134
Comanches, 135 - 158
Concho Rivers, 55, 74, 84, 165, 174
Conner, John, 147
Constance, Juliet, 139
Cordero (Chief), 136
Cordova, Vicente, 171
Crow Tribe, 89
Crowell, Sheriff L.C., 16
Custer, Gen. George Armstrong, 92, 96
D
Davis, Gov. Edmund, 98
De Gress, Gen. Jacob, 7
Deleon, Alonso43
Deno, Lottie, 63
DeVaca, Cabeza, 43,70-76
Diego de Guadalajara Expedition, 81
Dixie, Joe, 9
Dofflemyer, James, 174
Doneslson, Severn, 29
Dorantes, Andres, 71
Dorn, Van, 155
Dove Creek, 171
Drennan, John, 175
Duggan, Ed, 176
Duncan, John, 159
Durango, 168
E
Eagle Pass,15, 178
Edwards, Benjamin, 32,33
Edwards, Haden, 32

El Angel de Guarda, 84
El Mocho, 49 - 51
El Nacimento, 168, 177
Eldridge, Col. J.C., 147
Elliot, Maj. Joel H., 91
Espejo Expedition, 73
Estavanico, 71
F
Factor, Denbo, 14
Factor, Dindie, 9
Factor, Hardie, 9
Factor, Pompey, 8 - 10
Fannin, James, 34
Father Benavides, 80 - 82
Father Perea, 80, 81
Father Pinella, 43
Fay, Adams, 9
Felix, Josa, 31
Fields, Richard, 30 - 33
Fisher, John King, 15,16
Fisher-Miller Land Grant, 145
Flacco (Chief), 111,112,115
Flacco the Younger, 116,117
Ford, (Rip) John, 66,144
Fort Belknap, 59
Fort Bent, 93,94
Fort Chadbourne, 59
Fort Clark, 9,12,15
Fort Duncan, 6,9,10,159
Fort Griffin,59,63,118
Fort Johnson, 129
Fort Mason, 173
Fort Richardson, 98
Fort Sill, 101
Franciscan Mission of New Mexico, 80
G
Ganzabal, Wan Jose, 45
Gopher, John – John Horse, John Caballo, 2-4
Griner, Dallas, 17

Guest, N.T., 174
H
Harston, Emmor, 151,152
Hart, John F., 174
Hatch, Edward, 18
Hayes, Judge John, 139
Hays, Jack, 55, 115
Horcasitas, San Francisco Xavier de, 44
Horse, John, 5,6,7,16
Houston, Sam, 27 – 35, 112,117,137,143
Hunter, John D., 32,33
Huston, Felix, 141
I
Ildefonso, San, 44
Iron Shirt (Chief), 12
J
Jackson, I.E., 163
Jackson, Joshua, 163
Jackson, Louise, 163
Jackson, Lydia, 163
Jackson, Lyncoya, 29
Jackson, Moses, 163
Jackson, Pres. Andrew, 29,30
Jackson, Rebecca, 163
Jackson, Theodore, 29
Jenkins, B.F., 174,175
Jenkins, John H., 65
Jim Ned Creek, 163
Johnson (Chief), 60,61
Johnston, Albert Sidney, 35, 137,150
Jolly, John, 27
Jowers, W.G.W., 36
Juaregui, Atoio Maria, 170
Juarez, Benito, 4,6,171
July, Ben, 14
July, Billy, 14
Jumano Tribe, 69-88
Jumper, John, 3

K
Karankawa Tribe, 71
Kewiddawippa, 143,144
Kibbetts, Bobby, 9
Kibbetts, John, 7 – 10
Kickapoo Indians12, 167 - 176
Kickapoo Springs, 99,100
Kicking Bird, (Chief),17,90 - 93
King Phillip IV, 82
Kiowa Indians, 89 -107, 174
L
Lacy, Martin, 35,36
Lady in Blue, 81,82,86,87
LaJunta, 70,74 – 76, 84
Lamar, Mirabeau Bonaparte, 34,35,168,171
Lamar, Tabitha, 34
Lawson, J.L., 174
Lee, Capt. Arthur, 150
Linn, Johnny J., 138
Linnville, 54, 142
Lipan Apache45,51,109
Lipan Tribe, 109 - 120
Little Arkansas Treaty,91
Llano Estacada, 121,124
Lone Wolf (Chief), 13,90,93,95,99
Lone Wolf Mountain, 99,100
Lone Wolf v. Hitchcock, 102
Long, James, 53
Loraine, TX, 99
Los Lingos River, 126
Los Moras River, 16
Luxan, 64
Lyons, Warren, 144
M
Mackenzie,Ranald, 12,18,60,62,100,177
Mamadyte, Lone Wolf the Younger, 99,100
Mann, G.B., 174

Marcy, Capt. Randolph B.,59,66
Matamoras170
Matthews, Joe, 64
Maximillan, Ferdinand, 4
Medicine Lodge Treaty, 91,102
Mendoza, Juan Dominquez, 84,85
Mercado Creek,140
Merrit, Lt. Col. Wesley, 10
Mescalero Apaches, 111,118
Meusebach, John, 144-150
Miller, Bob, 175
Mitchell, Margaret Kerr, 139
Molina, Miquel, 50
Moore, Col., 113
Mope-cho-cope (Chief), 149,153
Muerto, Carne, 144
Mukewater Creek, 163,165
Muns, Harvey, 101
N
Nacogdoches, 26,32,33
Native American Church,54,59
Neches River, 37,110
Neches Saline, 35
Neely, Bill. 151
Neighbors, Buck, 173,174
Neighbors, Richard, 60,62,153
New Madrid, 23
Nolan, Philips, 27
Norris, Col. James M., 164
Nuestra Senora de la Candelaria, 44
O
Oginaga, 75
Old Owl (Chief), 150,160
Onate, Don Juande, 122
Oretaga, Juan de, 81
Ortiz, Col. Diego, 49,50

Ozona, 99,100
P
Painted Rocks, 55 - 57
Palo Duro Canyon, 12, 62
Panfilo de Narvaez Expedition, 70
Parker, William, 143
Parks, John R., 174 - 176
Parrilla, Diego Ortiz, 48
Patterson, Don, 67
Pavon, Jose Maria, 27
Payne, Adam, 10, 17
Payne, Isaac10,17
Payne, Titus, 16
Pecos River, 13,126
Perry, Capt. Frank, 8
Perry, T.T.,153
Perryman, Lt. W.J., 164
Pfeiffer, Bishop Michael, 86
Placido (Chief), 52 – 60, 63,66,67
Plum Creek Battlem 54,141
Polk, Pres. James K., 143
Polly, Annie, 155,156
Polly, Ephraim, 155,156
Polly, Kate, 155,156
Polly, Katie, 155,156
Port Lavaca, 141
Presidio de San Luis de Amarillas, 48
Presidio LaBahia, 51,54
Presidio, 75
Priddy, T.J., 162,163,165
Q
Quitaque, TX, 126
R
Reagan, John H., 36
Red River War, 12,147,161
Redford, 75
Republic of Fredonia, 32,33
Ridge, John, 28

Rio Concho, 72, 74, 75
Rio Grande, 1-8,15,43,70-74,85,112,116.161,170,171
Robinson, James,140
Robles, Domingo Cabello y, 50
Roemer, Ferdinand,147
Ross, Shapley, 60,154
Ross, Sul, 60
Runnels, Gov. Hardin R., 160
Running Water, Tenn., 21
S
Sabeata, Juan, 84
Sac-Fox Agency, 65
Salas,Fray Quan, 79,80,81
San Angelo (St. Angela), TX, 84,86,162,175
San Antonio Courthouse Battle, 138
San Fernando de Mexico, 47
San Gabriel River, 43 – 48,112
San Marcos, TX, 67,76
San Saba Mission,110
San Saba Presidio, 48
San Saba River,37,45 – 49,109,136,160
San Xavier, 48
Santa Anna (Chief),143
Santa Anna Peak,151,153
Santa Cruz de Queretaro, 47
Santa Cruz de San Saba Mission,47
Satank, (Chief),91,96,97,98
Satanta (Chief),91,96,97,98
Scott, William,22,23
Scout, August,17
Seminole Nation,3,4
Shaw, Jim,146 – 149,154
Sheridan, Gen. Phillip H.,18,96,97
Sherman, Gen. William,97

Shields, John,18
Shoemaker,Lt.,175,176
Shot-In-the-foot,154
Shroeder, Eric,82,83
Sibley, Agent Dr. John,135,136
Sitting-in-the-saddle,99
Sloat, Benjamin,149
Smith, Robert W.,37
Smithwick, Noah,65,112 - 116
Snively, Jacob,128 - 130
South Concho River,162,173
T
Tankersley, Annie, 159, 165,167
Tankersley, Clara,162,165,174
Tankersley, George W., 162,165,174,176
Tankersley, George,159
Tankersley, Marcus D.L., 162
Tankersley, Mary, 165,167
Tankersley, Richard Franklin,159 – 177
Tankersley, Sarah, 162,163
Tankersley,Elizabeth, 159,162,165,167,174
Tankersley,Fayette, 162,165,166,176
Tasewah, Tseep, 143
Tawakoni Jim,154
Taylor, Richard,28
Teron, Capt. Felipe de Rabago Y, 45 - 46
Terreros, Pedro Romeio, 47
Terreros, Alonso Giraldo,47
Texas Rangers, 54,55,142,161
Thernon, Tom,116
Thomas, Maj. May George,62
Thompson, John,9
Throckmorton, Gov. J.W.,64
Tonkawa Tribe, 41 – 68,141

Toppah, Amber,104
Tosche, 49
Tuerto, Capt., 82
U
Ute Indians, 133
V
Van Camp, Lt. Cornelius, 155
Van Horn, Earl, 154
Victoria, TX, 138,139
W
Ward, John, 9,10,13
Watts, Hugh Oran, 140
Watts, Juliet, 141
White Horse, 93
Whitefield, J.W., 130
Wildcat, 170
Williams, John, 160,163
Wilson, Ben, 14
Windus, Claron "Gus"
Y
Yellow Wolf, Chief, 150
Z
Zaragosa, 118
Zeragoza, 167

www.ingramcontent.com/pod-product-compliance
Lightning Source LLC
Chambersburg PA
CBHW030005110426
42736CB00040BA/376